WARRIOR WOMEN

TURNING LIFE LESSONS INTO LEGACY

DESIRÉ CRUZ

JAYMIE CHAPPLE • ELIZABETH CRUZ • SANDRA CRUZ
NICKY CUESTA • ARIELLE DEVITO • KATIE ESCOBAR
REBECCA HALE • TIFFANY HARRIS • CATHERINE LANDSCHOOT
KATHY MINCER • BRIDGET QUERNS • WHITNEY MARIE
JESSICA ROMAN • KAREN WIGENT

Warrior Women

ISBN: 978-1-64810-246-2

Published by Perfect Publishing Co.

I dedicate this book to my mother, Marie Casillo.

You are the definition of a Warrior Woman.

Thank you for showing me what true resilience is.

CONTENTS

PREFACE

What makes a person a warrior? After some research, I found an answer that stood out to me in Psychology Today. It stated, "Warriors generally are associated with two kinds of courage: 1) the ability to fight to protect themselves, 2) setting goals and developing the strength and skills to accomplish them." (April, 2018)

Throughout the past couple years of my own transformational journey, I began getting intentional about expanding my network. Oddly, the circle of women who inspired me began to get smaller as I grew older and became a business owner. Like many women, my intuition spoke to me. I could sense that there were many others out there who were feeling disconnected and unsure of how to fix that.

I felt God calling me to create a book filled with the stories of many women who are the EXACT definitions of a warrior listed above. This book was shown to me as a tool that could be used to take one small step in the right direction. Through the process, a significant amount of disconnect was revealed. With no surprise, my intuition was right! I found many everyday heroic women! Together we agreed we had a calling placed on our lives. It drives us to act and to share our stories, our lessons learned from them, and the battles we overcame to the world.

God revealed insights to us through the process of sharing our stories. These insights included; moments of vulnerability, clarity, self-alignment, transparency, healing, and legacy.

This book magnified the importance and the responsibility we had to make sure our loved ones received our story from our perspectives tangibly.

Soon enough, it became clear that we could identify with each other's daily battles. We all juggled similar roles that required a certain level of daily grind; roles of being mothers, spouses, caregivers, and/or business owners. Yet, it highlighted the fact that these same daily battles were more likely to be won when God was our armor and we surrounded ourselves with other warrior women.

In the following pages, you will get to meet many warrior women. May their stories make you pause, and feel their battle scars. We pray you are reminded by reading this that you are loved through every battle life brings and that you too are a warrior. Most importantly, may you see God's love and reflection in each of our stories.

Chapter 1 – Rebecca Hale

"Stand firm then, with the belt of truth buckled around your waist, with the breastplate of righteousness in place, and with your feet fitted with the readiness that comes from the gospel of peace. In addition to all this, take up the shield of faith, with which you can extinguish all the flaming arrows of the evil one. Take the helmet of salvation and the sword of the Spirit, which is the word of God".
(Ephesians 6: 14-17)

BY THE GRACE OF GOLF

By the grace of golf, a tiny golf ball changed my life in eight months. There are many forms of therapy and healing. For me it took forty-five years to find my transformation tool: Golf. Let me tell you how swinging a golf club showed me how to put down my own trauma armor and start each day engaging the Armor of God (Ephesians 6:10-17).

Personally, I experienced childhood trauma at the hands of church people whom I trusted. My own repressed trauma resurfaced quite some time ago. I didn't have the tools to deal with the memories or shame. I went to therapy and many healers who would help me shift my emotions and make me feel better, temporarily. Kind of a band-aid for the situation…I would feel safe in those spaces to talk about things and let the memories resurface. I would feel better and then I would return to my life and my armor would go right back into place. I would armor up to face the world but wasn't getting to the root cause or healing at a cellular level.

Humans are resilient and can have quite remarkable coping and adaptability skills but, these skills can come at great cost. What once helped for survival generally doesn't help for thriving. For me, when I was on, I was on. When I wasn't, it was bad. I would often hibernate or avoid taking action or making self-destructive decisions. Committing to plans in the future was a recipe for disaster...who knew what state I would be in when the day came to show up and follow through on a commitment? I struggled showing up for my boys emotionally when they needed me most and I was unable to formulate healthy friendships and romantic partnerships.

Finally, I had to surrender to the truth that I was safe and no longer in danger. I realized that I was often responding with an automatic response based on previous experiences. I had to ask for help. I started deliberately asking God to watch over me: to armor me up. Every morning, I would start by speaking the Armor of God into the mirror. Eventually, I started asking people I trusted to be there for me. I began to realize that we are not intended to go it alone. I began trusting God, others and myself.

Then came golf. As a lifelong athlete, I used to see golf as a sedentary "sport". I just didn't get it. Yet, the first time I completed a full round of golf, I walked off the 18th green into the women's locker room and bawled my eyes out, not because I was terrible (and oh, was I terrible!). No, it wasn't that. You see, trauma is held in our bodies and can be released with movement. That first game of golf tapped into my vast reserve of unhealed trauma.

At first, I struggled with my golf game. My physical armor of tight muscles and fascia had served me well in other athletic endeavors. I was pretty fit and the muscular tone was supportive of my efforts. However, my physical armor (my protective fight or flight response) was not conducive to a fluid, repeatable golf swing.

Then I had an awakening. The repetitive rotational demand of the swing and the patience and persistence of my golf partner (my boyfriend), unlocked the severe trauma tension in my body. Technically speaking, I had so much trauma tension in my body that in order for me to swing the club I had to defy the mechanics of the swing. I had to teach my body to relax to allow the fluidity of movement needed for a consistent and successful swing.

I was standing on the tee box, and up until this point, I'd been swinging my club like a baseball bat. My boyfriend, with his analytical engineering mind, had been watching the levers of my body, which didn't resemble anything close to a golf swing. Finally, he couldn't take it anymore. He stepped up behind me, put his hands on my hips, and led me through the timing of my lower body and the separation of my upper body needed to create a golf swing. WHAT?! My athletic body had absolutely no recall of this kind of movement, which was completely foreign to my body.

This purposeful, guided supported movement unlocked something very deep within me. This is when I learned that my physical body had acted like an armor of protection for the past thirty years of my life. My muscles and connective tissues were constantly engaged: always on guard for danger. I found my relaxation in an activity out in nature... on the golf course.

I have learned the following strategies:

- First, golf helped me recognize my trauma response which was engaging my muscular armor.
- Second, I recruited a supportive, trusted person who helped me recognize when I was responding from past traumas. Having someone help you identify and shift your physiological response in the moment is very powerful.
- Third, based on this new awareness, create a new routine to stop and shift out of my fight or flight response.
- Lastly, I learned to practice being disciplined to consciously create new responses.

The same transformation would not have happened if I'd taken lessons with a golf pro. My relationship gave me a "safe space" and my body was able to relax. I had permission, and gentle, hands-on instruction that elicited a new experience. A round of golf on an 18 hole course is 72 strokes for par, and includes 2 distinct activities (to keep it simple) swinging a club to send a ball flying down the fairway and putting on the green. The golf swing requires a demanding rotational movement. For me, the repetition of this movement over 100 times caused my muscles to fatigue and ultimately allowed my body to relax for a successful swing. In contrast, putting requires zero rotational movement and a quiet, relaxed body. Tension in your body while putting will not allow you to effectively gauge the finesse needed to effectively putt. In the beginning, I was repeating these 2 activities over 144 times and playing a full round of golf gave me four hours out in nature to practice shifting my physiological response (from fight or flight to rest and digest).

Since that first experience, my understanding of the transformational power of golf has deepened. I learned how to deal with stress in my golf game, and then, I experienced a carry over effect away from the golf course. I began to hold myself accountable for how my stress showed up in my interactions with people.

Ideally, my little ball and I would start at the first tee box. If we were lucky enough, the two of us would journey all 18 holes together. However it is far more likely that the particular ball (and a few others, as well) will not make it the whole way (water hazard, the same water hazard, the woods, someone's backyard, a different water hazard). This relationship with the ball demands (and cultivates!) patience, poise, a keen sense of body awareness, and my total presence. Throughout this 18-hole journey, I have the possibility of experiencing the entire range of human emotions. I have seen and expressed them all!

One example of these very insightful experiences occurred as a result of a bunker shot. A bunker shot (out of a sand trap) is not the easiest shot, especially for a beginner. So, I don't usually have high expectations to get out of the bunker with a great deal of success. This particular time, I attempted to hit the sand, behind the ball, like you are supposed to and sadly the ball remained safely snuggled in the sand...untouched, which is every golfer's nightmare! In that moment, I felt a surge of rage flow through my body. I had already had six months of experiencing my emotions splashing out on the course. My primary objective out on the course was to learn how, in the moment, I can be aware of and shift the response of my nervous system. I was learning how to be in control of the automatic response I had to anger, frustration, and stress. I didn't have a terribly external expression of my rage but this moment was one of the most intense sensations I have ever experienced internally within my body. I was fully present with it.

Exploring the movements and mindset of golf helped me to:

- Gain insight to how my nervous system is hijacked by past experiences both on and off the course
- Explore my physical limitations of flexibility, balance and strength
- Learn the importance of creating a sense of safety with trusted people
- Establish effective tools and routines to release emotions that improved my consistency on the golf course and enable loving connections

Now, I teach these four points to my clients and students. Professionally, I've worked over 25 years with people of all ages to heal them both physically and emotionally through body movement. I was really good at recognizing other people's strategies for handling trauma long before I figured out how to handle my own trauma response. Through my own experience, as well as working with others, I've gained first-hand knowledge and insight about how trauma impacts behavior, movement and connection.

Trauma is not predictable. The type of trauma I am speaking of cannot be seen on the outside. When trauma resurfaces — and it can show up at the most inopportune times — it can incapacitate you and leave you in a chronic state of hypervigilance. But trauma doesn't have to be Trauma with a capital "T." The cumulative effects of small daily traumas (also known as Life!) can also build up to unhealthy levels and cause you to respond defensively in the present moment. Trauma can make you numb and make you pursue addictive behaviors such as excessive workouts, compulsive and destructive eating habits, drinking or drugging to avoid feeling anything.

Golf has given me a fun playground (a sandbox!) to practice how to shift out of my fight or flight state — to go from surviving to thriving. No matter how bad a particular shot is, there is ALWAYS the possibility for redemption and renewal. There's always a do-over. There's always an invitation to presence...and an invitation to live fully in this moment.

If golf is not your thing, you can find these same insights through dance, yoga, hiking, swimming, biking and other physical activities that require rotational movement. Even music, painting or horseback riding create movement in the body that releases emotions. For me, the breakthrough was having to consciously pay attention to how my body was responding in the moment. I had to relinquish my armor to be successful at golf. What a blessing!

Lessons and experiences in golf can be applied to life off the golf course.

1) Recognize your impact on the ball — The golf ball has a tough exterior that can withstand the impacts of multiple golf swings, even those of professional golfers which can exceed 100 mph. But its behavior can be erratic, if you, as the steward, do not apply presence, patience and self-regulation.

- In life, take responsibility for how you show up in relationships to cultivate love and connection instead of disconnect and distance.

2) Your environment, chosen or not, is not controllable. The golf course provides an unpredictable canvas. There are rolling hills, sloping fairways, trees, water features, bunkers and even the occasional house. In addition, you could have hot, cold, wind or even rain. You can choose whether you play in these types of weather conditions but even in perfect conditions the golf course will give you unpredictable surprises.

- In life, when you can choose the environment you enter, and still you will be surrounded by temptations and challenges. Take time to notice how your environment impacts upon you and those you love.

3) Leave the past behind. You get 14 clubs in your bag which, if struck well, produce varying distances. One mis-hit on any given hole is no big deal. As long as you take a deep breath and get present with yourself and the ball, you can get right back on track. However, as a good friend of mine says, you are free to play "angry girl" golf in which case it is likely that no club will be your friend.

- In life, if we continue to bring our past to new experiences we can ruin a beautiful connection.

4) Failure is guaranteed. What a blessing to know that you will never be perfect on the course. Professional golfers arent perfect and playing golf is their job. They practice many hours every day, multiple days a week. If you watch a tournament, you can bear witness to their squabbles.

- In life, failure is necessary for growth. The key is to get back up and try again with new insights. None of us arrived with a script. We are all unique and will have our own journey.

These lessons can manifest themselves in many other activities. Find an activity that inspires you to admire the contrast of your environment and how participation makes you feel.

Appreciate the present moment and be grateful for the opportunity to take chances and make mistakes. Love and enjoy the experiences of your human experience. Remember, we are all stewards in this journey called life. Each of us is blessed with purpose and meaning. We rise to the occasion when we live in the present moment, connected and living in our true God given integrity.

About the Author

Rebecca Hale has been a lifelong resident outside of Boston, Massachusetts. Her greatest joy has been raising her 2 young men. She has enjoyed a career as a pediatric physical therapist. She enjoys exploring nature in the woods, ocean and on the golf course.

Chapter 2 – Jaymie Chapple

*"No matter what people tell you, words
and ideas can change the world."*
– Robin Williams

"MISS INDEPENDENT IS TOO DRIVEN"

What major life event started your transformation? Do you empathize with women that have undergone traumatic, life altering events? Have you experienced incidents that shape your life much like the mountains shape the valleys?

I have, and for me I'd have to say my transformation began in 2006. At that time, I was working full time as a Registered Nurse in the ICU and working part time as a clinical nursing instructor at the local community college. I had just completed my under-graduate studies and obtained my BSN that year as well. My husband and I were dedicated to the growth of our business. I became all too familiar with multitasking, maintaining a busy life, successfully filling the role of co-owner of a small business, mom, student, wife and Nurse. I was being molded by the everyday elements that I had been exposed to.

There were a series of events that had shaped who I am today. In 2004 I lost my brother unexpectedly on my birthday.

Just two short years later I would have to grieve the loss of my cousin. My cousin was more like a little brother. This loss was incredibly painful, we were close. He had been tragically killed in a hit and run. This incident happened to fall on my sister's birthday. To me loss is not always finite or tangible for that matter. It is a feeling of deprivation or that of profound grief that can last an infinite period of time.

I was devastated, two lives taken too soon. For some time following these tragedies, celebrating birthdays and holidays was very difficult for me. I recall both of these days vividly. "Why?" I asked God? Two near and dear people to me, "why so soon?"

I couldn't make sense of the losses, unfathomable on so many levels. My cousin would never meet his daughter. My brother would never have the opportunity to explore adulthood; he was only 20 years old. With these losses there were some gains. The old adage is true "what goes up must come down and vice versa." That following Father's Day of 2007, I was blessed with some incredible news, I learned that I was expecting my fourth child.

For the most part, I was trusting and naïve, but I still thrived in challenging myself day to day. The very fiber of my being was to approach life with utmost intention and to be a productive citizen. During this pregnancy I decided to pursue my MS in FNP (Family Nurse Practitioner). I also held a full time position at a Skilled Nursing Facility and continued my work as a clinical adjunct nursing instructor. During my time in the clinical setting with students I was scouted by the Dean of a private college.

As the driven, multitasker, and master at most everything I did, I dove in and accepted a full time job as Associate Professor at the College. I had resigned my two other positions. This was how I functioned best, how I excelled. I had managed my new career and changed my degree to MS in Education, which was necessary to satisfy the requirements to hold tenure. This was no small feat, I graduated in 2011 as a Nurse Educator with honors and continued to work full time, co-owner of a small business, mother, and wife.

At the time I felt I had it all. My losses were not forgotten but I was still going to succeed in all that I did. I spent nearly 7 years as a college professor and loved the direction that my life had taken. I was abundant with the riches that life had to offer. I was able to manage a great deal as a driven woman and as part of a team.

We know that loss inevitably leads to change. In self-reflection, I asked myself, "Was I a mountain or a river?" Up to this point in my life I identified as a mountain, steadfast in my ways, only briefly molded by the elements that I had been exposed to. A mountain in that I was convicted in what I believed to be true, almost rigid in my ways. Inflexible with my moral compass. My family and my career are and will always be priority. Having said this, I had recognized that I had not processed my losses and hardships thoroughly. I spent so much time keeping busy and managing a wealth of tasks which would have not permitted me to learn and grow as a person from my losses. This had come at a heavy cost and it was about to become evident. I likely overlooked some important lessons early on as well. Lessons that would later be revealed.

In 2013 my unraveling began. I had undergone a life changing experience, which probably would have knocked many women in my position down for the count. I was absolutely humiliated, my husband, presumed life partner, and business partner had asked me for a divorce out of the blue. He expressed that "I was too driven, too independent." My marriage had come to an end. I was a newly single mom of 4. How was I going to manage? We had just built our home the month prior. I still recall the feelings of excitement that we had built this life and home together. I felt I was being punished for my successes. None of this made sense to me, it all left me feeling blindsided and confused.

So many changes, the world was shifting under my feet. What once felt safe and secure was no longer either of those. I was certainly not steady on my feet. I spent about a week feeling distraught and ambivalent. My anxiety was at an all-time high. I had been barraged, shamed. I was left feeling helpless. At one point, I will never forget, I was retching while in the pantry, a moment of weakness. My husband at the time walked in on me getting sick. Instead of comforting me he threw a waste basket and said "stop being so dramatic." "Go take your crazy pill." For me having anxiety and managing it came with being harassed. This was a surreal and humiliating moment for me. I meant nothing to him, I was nauseated, we had four children together but that did not matter to him. This pain I was feeling was immeasurable. I felt destroyed. I second guessed my being, my self–worth.

It is reasonable to say I was not well represented and had sustained a great unjust loss. We had built a life together and the provisions of our divorce were one sided but I could not afford an attorney to represent my best interests. Part of me still loved him and believed that all would work out. The divorce ultimately did not end in my favor but the details do not matter at this point.

I felt as though my world as I once knew it was forever gone. I had to manage sharing time with our children. Manage bills on my own. I had to manage child care for my three children and managed supporting them with their sports when they were with me. I no longer had the support or a partner. I had to learn to manage alone, not rely on anyone else. There was no team, it was me. It was quickly overwhelming.

Recognizing that I was alone and had very little time to feel pity, I pulled my bootstraps up. It did not take me long to change my perspective. I had to be a warrior woman, mom, and full time professor, and this was exactly what I was going to do. As a person, I was raw for some time. I was sensitive to most everything, I cried daily. This was to be expected. Despite the heartbreak, I had gained so much more once I leveraged my tragedy into an opportunity.

I started to take better care of myself, exercising and engaging in hobbies. I sought out daily goals and enjoyed my day to day accomplishments. Getting myself to work and my kids to school were accomplishments that I appreciated. I was no longer seeking acceptance from others. I had accepted myself and I was not going to chase relationships or friendships. I had recognized quickly that if I didn't pull myself together I could very well lose it all. My children were looking to me for guidance and strength and that was exactly what I intended to do. I could only allow myself to grieve for so long.

In 2014 I welcomed my fifth child into this world. What a beautiful moment meeting her was. As a single mom I was scared but knew I had to continue to show strength. This change was not of loss but of survival. I had to adapt to being a single mom of 5 in a relatively short period of time.

During November of 2015 I was still employed at the college as a nursing professor. I had been managing it all, or so I thought. Much had transpired over the years and contributed to my slow but progressive decline. I had my first diagnosed panic attack. Have you ever felt a crushing panic? Heart palpitations so intense you literally feel the pulse in your ears? A panic attack is a feeling of unease and doom. I don't wish panic disorder or anxiety on anyone because it can cause momentary paralysis, at least it has for me. I will never forget Thanksgiving eve of that year. I had an experience that left me feeling violated. You see at the time, I pushed through the pain, I had a holiday to celebrate and my children were looking for strength and normalcy from me. I cried on my way home but I had to tend to my family and prepare for the holiday. Not processing the experience in a healthy way would later be evident.

It had taken 4 months for me to recover, to feel safe, somewhat whole again in a covert fashion. I had experienced trauma and compartmentalized what had happened. The experience had resulted in some setbacks. The unresolved trauma and losses caught up with me. I was unable to continue my current position at the college, untreated trauma can have devastating consequences. Inability to concentrate and focus were some of the consequences I had experienced. Once again I experienced a loss; but at the same time I had to trust in the medical professionals. My anxiety had stunned me and I was unable to concentrate on work. I had to take some time to heal. I was feeling ashamed. Another loss coupled with the stigma that surrounds mental illness. Those that have mental illness cannot control the onset of their condition any more than a person diagnosed with cancer. Unfortunately, mental illness is often laden with stigma. Mental wellness is vastly important for overall well-being. Some may even delay treatment out of fear of being ostracized.

What was I going to do? I had to do my best to be responsive, intentional with my every move. I had to accept that I had to put my passion of being a college professor aside, at least for now. I had to treat my anxiety. Over the next few years I had decided to dabble in some home care, care management and critical care nursing. I was blessed to have my niece come to stay with me during these years. She became more like a daughter to me. I couldn't bear to disappoint any of my children. I had to survive.

Until March of 2019 I was managing. I had hit rock bottom at that point. The trauma I had encountered previously had been tucked away but not forgotten. On March 26th I had lost my step mother to depression. I would like to think that she fought hard but I felt guilty for some time. The seriousness of mental health disorders hit home. I was in utter shock that she was in such a bad place that I had not recognized the depths of her despair. I was angry, and felt the burden of survivor's guilt that many survivors feel. I have anxiety, why did God spare me and take her? Why does mental illness have to be so taboo?

Within weeks of her passing I had encountered a situation at work. I had been harassed and this triggered another full on panic attack. I couldn't physically even enter the workplace. I couldn't make myself get out of my car. You see, the connection of the incidents was so strong. This time I knew that I needed to seek professional help early on. I had collaborated with health professionals and followed the plan of care. It was not easy, I had to fight with everything in me. I had to maintain my home, care for my 6 children. I was out of work for nearly five months. At the time I had fixed income with limited family support. I am grateful for a few, my sister Candy helped me in more ways than one. My desire to get well again far outweighed the fear of taking "a crazy pill."

Once again the losses forced me to re-examine who I was. "Was I a mountain or a river? " These experiences were trying yet I rose every day. My children were my greatest responsibility and pride. I needed to not only be physically present but I needed to show them strength and resilience. I was a warrior woman. Through a great deal of change and loss I had emerged in a matter of a few years. I underwent therapy and leaned on some choice family and friends. Unfortunately in my experience divorce and trauma contributed to the loss of friends and the strain of some relationships.

I told myself, not only was I going to survive, I was going to rise, thrive and level up. I dug deep to the depths of my soul. So much that I had felt an emotional connection with myself that I had never experienced before. A connection that only few are blessed or brave to embrace. I say this because I no longer expected or hoped that others would feel or see me the way I desired. I realized self-worth. What others thought of me no longer mattered to me. My clan of friends and family had been more protected but was markedly smaller in quantity. The emotional strength and courage that I gained ultimately provided guidance for my kids.

My ability to reflect and learn from my life lessons along the way is the legacy I leave for my children. I hope that they have courage to forgive, to adhere to their morals and self-reflect. I had discovered that in order to provide them with security I couldn't do that unless I forgave myself and others for their wrong doings. I recognized that I had limits, that I was worthy. Some may even say that the ability to self-reflect is my superpower.

And so once again I journeyed through the healing process. I put one foot forward and the other followed. The first step is always the most difficult. Anxiety may be a condition recognized in the DSM but for me it was a culmination of events which had permeated my life beyond my control and led me to where I am today. If I could teach my children anything or even my students, I would want them to know the difference between what they can and cannot control, realistically. It is human nature to want to seek validation and control. Anxiety is thought to stem from a lack of control. I urge you to put one foot forward and the other will follow.

How did I recognize this and why did it take me more than 4 decades to do so? Who is this beautiful person? Once I was able to embrace my abilities and limitations I was fulfilled, markedly happier. What had resonated with me through my healing was that this "strong, independent and too driven" woman was beautiful and deserved "earned happiness." That is right, "earned happiness." True happiness does not just appear, it takes work and commitment to sustain any longevity. Like many women, I did not focus my energies where I should have earlier and that I was far too trusting. These were life lessons for me.

Although there were some hardships through this journey every person I encountered or had as a friend taught me something. Some lessons were more painful than others. I no longer look back in disbelief or disappointment in some of my decisions, they were mine. Much like a river shapes the valleys and mountains, I love who I am becoming. I embrace the strong, independent, too driven woman. I have so much to be grateful for. I have my family, my health, my home, and my career. I am no longer looking at "what ifs and why nots". I am placing my focus on what I can and will do, scripting my own destiny.

I had tremendous growth during such a short period of time. I endured loss but I gained so much more in the end. My children, for the most part, adore me. Many women might have given up on themselves rendering them unable to care appropriately for their children. Some might even self-destruct had they experienced the losses that I have. I came close to this but gained strength through my children. When I forgave myself and others, I grew as a person and that and self- reflection. I also found having faith was instrumental as well. Faith in whatever higher being I believe in. For me my faith is more about my moral compass and treating others as I'd like to be treated.

In January 2020, in the rise of the pandemic I felt I had the most control that I had in many years as a result of my transformation. I was approached online by a mutual friend. I was apprehensive and reserved to allow a relationship to grow initially. It was important to me to build a solid friendship with him. I did not even talk on the phone with him until 2 weeks before we met. Up until then our conversations were strictly on social media. By the time we started talking and I heard his voice we had developed a connection. The connection was deep, the chemistry we had was undeniable. We decided to meet later that spring.

Early in our courtship I knew that I had found my life partner. I had developed a relationship with someone that would compliment me, not compliment me. I gained self confidence in the years leading up to this through my hardships. These events provided a solid foundation for the romance to flourish. What I desired now was a partner, an equal that added substance to my life. We had created shared goals just three months into our relationship. We had been transparent with our experiences in both hardship and loss. This enhanced our abilities to establish boundaries and expectations. This may sound harsh or even scripted, but for us it was necessary for our success as a team. We had independently spent years working on ourselves and then our paths crossed, shaping the platform of our lives together. We enrich each other's lives, we feel very strongly that is how it should be. If you want you could have this too.

In April of 2021 we decided to make it official. We were married July 2 2022, surrounded by our close friends and loved ones. During the process of planning the wedding we had grown fond of the idea of working side by side. We enjoy one another's company so much that it is our end goal. We have merged our passions and skills together and started our own business making wooden flower arrangements. We both enjoy crafting the creations.

Throughout the wedding planning we had experienced some hardships. My husband's children chose not to be part of our wedding day. It was and always will be a sore spot for me. Did they not accept me or their father's choice to marry me?

It was still a beautiful day, just a piece of me was missing. The pain my husband felt still haunts me. I feel the weight of burden yet I am grateful to be married today. I will be honest, I was scared. I feared he would choose not to marry me. Despite his jokes that I'd leave him at the Altar, stakes were higher for me that he would leave me there. Here we are going strong, 7 months later happily married and engaged with our children. Love surpasses guilt and shame.

During all of this in March of 2022 my dad fell ill and was diagnosed with cancer, is an alcoholic and what I can only assume to be suffering from depression. I am his primary caregiver. Unfortunately my father is resistant to seeking psychological evaluation or help. But I know depression, after all I had lost my stepmom to it. Much has happened since with my dad. Tragedy and trials were experienced, painful words were exchanged. At this point in my life I felt I was much better equipped to manage these hardships that I had endured with him. Loss of person not of life. Loss of what I once knew, an acceptance of what was to come. I forgive, I understand, and have unconditional love for him and more importantly for me.

All too often as a woman I would fear change, fear the unknown. As women we are historically and arguably less predictable than our counterparts. Let's face it, we live, love and grow all the while making men guess as to what our next move is. Embrace it. This is a sign of a true warrior.

I will leave you with this, tragedies can be leveraged into opportunities. Anxiety doesn't define me. I urge all women to approach life with vigor and be intentional every day. Through my journey I have and will continue to grow as a person. I have learned that it is safe for me to be vulnerable. I also plead to women to defend themselves against violations to any degree. I continue my work as a full time nurse, homeowner, newlywed, and mom. I am the happiest, most wholesome me that I can be. I am a river. I am flexible, I tend to nourish others along the way. I shape the landscape and lend direction to those who I encounter. I am a leader. This is me, driven, strong and independent. This is my life story of both loss and resilience.

About the Author

Jaymie is a newlywed, mother of 8 who lives in the Finger Lakes Region. She is a nurse by day. Her hobbies include making wooden flowers, exercising and traveling. She is also a Netflix junkie and is always wanting a good drama to enjoy. Her business is Magnolia Craft 0702 in which she creates custom wooden flower arrangements for all occasions. She would be happy to create long-lasting arrangements for you.

Chapter 3 – Bridget Querns

I GUESS YOU WON'T MIND

Great lions can find peace in a cage.
But we should only do that
as a last
resort.
So those bars I see that restrain your wings,
I guess you won't mind
if I pry them
open.

– Rumi

"HEART FAILURE"

Nothing about my final pregnancy was expected. "After having three children in six years, you would think you'd know how babies are made," people joked. That wasn't the point. My husband, Alex, and I were intentional about our physical relationship because we knew it probably wasn't safe for me to carry another pregnancy.

With two of our first three children, I had experienced preeclampsia. This is a condition that can develop during pregnancy and is characterized by high blood pressure and protein in the urine. Preeclampsia can result in damage to multiple organs including the kidneys, liver, lungs, heart, and eyes, and may also cause a stroke or other brain injury. We had decided that we were content with our family of five and didn't want to risk my life, as this condition can be fatal for both the mother and child.

We don't have any explanation for how I got pregnant with Avery. We say that he must have been God's plan, and if that's the case, God's plan did not look the way *I* would imagine it. Since I was concerned for our health from the beginning, I took every precaution necessary. If my doctor made a suggestion, I listened.

When I tell you I tried everything, that is no exaggeration. I have always had a fear of needles. I'm the type of person who faints when I see blood, let alone have my own blood drawn. I was so determined to stay healthy for this baby and my family that I even tried acupuncture. Talk about NEEDLES! And when one of those tiny little hair-thin suckers hits a nerve… ZING!

Not for lack of trying to stay healthy, I ended up hospitalized at 34 weeks pregnant with severe preeclampsia. I don't know whether I'm proud or ashamed to say my boss had to urge me to go to the hospital. It was out of character for him to play the concerned colleague, so I knew I must have really appeared ill.

This was my second trip to the hospital in two days. My midwife had met me at the hospital the day before to run some tests because of my high blood pressure readings and constant headache. Ultimately, she had decided it was safe to send me home. I was hesitant to go again because I didn't want to be labeled the "needy" patient.

Please, don't ever avoid seeking medical care because you're afraid of being judged. I strongly encourage advocating for yourself or asking a trusted person to help you do so. My decision to return to the hospital may have saved my life.

When I got to the labor and delivery unit, I was quite surprised to find out that my doctor wanted me admitted right away. Of course, I hadn't prepared for this scenario. Like I said, nothing about this pregnancy was anticipated. My family was also alarmed by the news that I had been admitted to the hospital. I don't remember how they made it work when, all of a sudden, mom wasn't going to be there for an undetermined length of time. We all had more questions than answers.

There I was, the only person in the postpartum unit who was still *very* visibly pregnant. At least they let me wear my own pajamas instead of that scratchy, cold hospital gown that barely covers anything. If I thought I'd had it rough with the needles before, I was in for a treat. Acupuncture was a JOY compared to the thick-as-jelly injections of steroids they were giving me in my swollen, purple thighs. *It's all for the baby*, I would tell myself every time I fought to breathe as the nurse stabbed me again.

Two days after I'd been admitted, I'd had multiple rounds of medications I couldn't remember. I was still suffering from headaches that made it difficult to see straight. My medical team was confident that our baby had received enough steroids to strengthen his lungs, and weighed that against my deteriorating health. They made the decision to induce labor.

Most of the following 32 hours were a blur. It felt like everyone was moving so quickly, yet I was stuck in a cloud thanks to the magnesium sulfate dripping into my IV. Among the side effects I recall, my head felt like a balloon. At times, if I tried to stand or walk, my muscles would work very slowly, or I'd feel quite weak. I may have slurred my words. I was confused, and frankly, I was terrified. My nurse had said I was receiving this medication to prevent a stroke. I don't know how any person could process that information effectively while enduring the pain of labor.

Thirty-two hours.

That's how long I allowed my body to fight. I have to believe my innate bodily wisdom was not going to allow this child to be born until he was ready. At barely 35 weeks of gestation, even my cells knew he wasn't ready. Exhausted and sleep deprived, I made the decision to take a break from the Pitocin they'd used to induce labor. I just wanted to know if my body would do what we needed it to on its own.

As soon as they shut off the medication, my uterus stopped contracting. I asked my midwife if she honestly thought more Pitocin and more time would result in a successful delivery. Though she believed it would, something deep within me said *NO*.

My intuition was so firm, I listened like I had no other choice. I would later find out that magnesium sulfate can cause respiratory depression in newborns who may even require resuscitation in the delivery room as a result of its use. I don't want to know what would have happened if Avery had been exposed to it any longer. I wish I had been fully informed about the dangers as well as benefits of attempting labor, but I am ultimately grateful I listened to my inner wisdom.

I was going to deliver this baby on my terms, even if nothing else was under my control. I took a peaceful moment with my family to meditate, pray, and gather myself. We asked to meet with the anesthesiologist and surgeon so we could formulate a plan as a team. My fear of needles was looming large as I had experienced a cesarean section before and knew what spinal anesthesia entailed.

I gathered every bit of peace I could muster and focused on my breath. In just minutes, my baby would be in my arms, or so I thought. Sitting on the edge of the operating table, I slumped into a nurse's chest.

The anesthesiologist fished for the correct location to deliver the numbing medication. "Can you shift your back just a bit to the left?" he asked. I was already feeling the familiar wave of nausea and warmth. My ears were ringing, and my vision was narrowing to a tunnel of light. I willed my body to shift, urging myself to remain present and conscious. I knew they'd found the spot because my legs began to drift to sleep, the heaviness crawling up my body.

There's no good way to explain the feeling of lying *so exposed* on an operating table during a c-section. It's another level of nakedness to be conscious of the fact that strangers are looking at you inside out, carefully moving around your inner organs, and you're awake for every moment of it. Everyone's focus was on me, yet I was completely separated from the commotion, a blue surgical shroud obscuring my view.

Only moments seemed to pass before Avery was lifted to earthside. It was unusually quiet. His little cries were weak, and when they brought him to my side, his skin was an unnerving blue. Again, my gut told me something wasn't right. The recovery room was silent and dimly lit. I deeply felt the chasm of separation between myself and my sweet new baby. I should have been warming him skin to skin. Instead, I was shuddering as the spinal medication wore off. I would learn in the recovery room that Avery had suffered respiratory distress. He was receiving the highest level of breathing support available in the special care nursery.

Avery continued to get stronger and healthier, but my recovery was not as encouraging. Shortly after returning to my postpartum room, I experienced chest tightness and shortness of breath. Thankfully, my sister was present and immediately called the nursing station. A chest x-ray confirmed pulmonary edema (excessive fluid in my chest cavity) following severe preeclampsia. I learned that day that preeclampsia remains just as dangerous during the postpartum period as it does during pregnancy. However, when my team gave me the green light to go home, I was thrilled. Why would I question them?

Just five days after Avery was born, I couldn't ignore how terrible I felt. It was beyond the expected new parent fatigue. I had another vice-grip headache, my blood pressure would not go down, and I was very concerned. Again, we headed to the hospital – me, my husband, and our tiny new baby. Unlike most emergency room experiences, once the triage team evaluated me, we were whisked back to a private room. I figured it was because they didn't want our newborn exposed to sick people. I quickly found out this was not the case. A team of medical staff surrounded me in a flurry of activity as soon as I sat down.

Within minutes, there were so many wires attached to me that I felt like a science experiment. They administered round after round of blood pressure medication, but my heart did not want to cooperate. After the last round, the nurse left the room and closed the door behind her. It felt as though no one had said a word to us the entire time they were working, and now, it was eerily still and quiet. I just wanted someone to let us in on the secret. Why was everyone so frantic, and why had no one told us what was going on?

As the questions rattled in my brain, another woman opened the door and poked her head in. I'll never forget the words she spoke or the monotone way in which she delivered them. I don't even know who she was addressing.

"It's heart failure."

I never could have anticipated how I would respond when faced with such a grave diagnosis. Against all expectations, I felt peace. At that moment I was so certain everything was ok - *more* than ok. Everything was serenely right in the world. My family was safe and cared for. *I* was safe and cared for. I felt so close to my Creator that I could palpably sense the reassuring pulse and warmth of the God who loved me into being.

THIS is the peace that surpasses all understanding. There was no room for fear. An overflowing love filled that little room.

After every medical intervention had failed, my body finally responded to a different kind of intervention. There was no long recovery period. There were no signs of damage to my heart. The doctors couldn't explain what happened.

When you've come that close, not to death, but to the Divine, you cannot help but reorient your entire life in response. In the ensuing months and years, I left the job that I'd held for a decade and closed a very profitable business. I made it my mission to reacquaint myself with my soul's purpose. Clearly, God had a reason for sending me a frightening wake-up call.

The hibernation period of the pandemic urged me into reflective solitude. The isolation felt divinely timed, delivered at just the moment when I undertook my soul's deepest work. I asked myself who I came here to be. What unique strengths did I possess in order to fulfill that calling? How could I restructure my life in honor of the gift of clarity I'd received? This is an ongoing process. I am emerging more every day, healing decades of fear, pain, and confusion so I can fully activate my soul's potential.

I want to leave you with a short story that centers around an image God showed me during this process – a mirror.

You have been gifted a priceless ornamental mirror. You choose the perfect spot for your mirror. As you hang it, you run your hands over its ornately carved frame, appreciating the skill and time someone put into this handiwork. You love the way it expands and brightens the space you've hung it in. When you look into this mirror, you're amazed by the way it seems to reflect not just your image, but who you really are at your core.

Others notice this new addition and are in awe of how well it complements the space. It is almost as though this mirror was always meant to hang right here. It's like it was made for exactly this spot. The mirror captivates attention like a fine work of art, reflecting the unique beauty of every observer.

Over time, the mirror gets ignored, though it continues to be just as lovely as when you first hung it. Dust builds up. It gets bumped, knocked down, and scratched. Eventually, you remove it from the wall and store it in the basement to prevent further damage. After a particularly brutal storm, your basement floods, covering everything in it in a muddy, moldy film. You're devastated. You feel guilty for having left the mirror in such a careless place, even though you were just trying to protect it.

You resolve to treat it better and set out to find someone who can restore it. This isn't a job for just anyone - this requires a master craftsperson. The mirror is, after all, still a priceless treasure.

YOU are a priceless treasure.

You have gone to great lengths to protect yourself from the onslaught of the world's devastating realities. To no avail, you've hidden yourself away, hoping this would save you from the pain of getting knocked down. But you wear the world's wounds, and you feel as though this makes you less lovely, less worthy of love.

Friend, everything about you makes you lovely. There is no shame in asking for the master craftsperson's help so you can recognize yourself again. When you have wiped away the gunk that obscures your radiant glow, you'll realize it's not just your own reflection you see, but the reflection of God within you.

Please, don't wait to listen to your heart until it is failing you.

About the Author

Bridget Querns is a soul-centered coach and host of the podcast Passionate Pursuits. She believes activating our potential leads us to a life of wholeness. She, her partner, and her four children live in upstate New York. You can learn more about working with Bridget here.

Chapter 4 – Sandra Cruz

"And He said to me, 'My grace is sufficient for you, for My strength is made perfect in weakness.'"
2nd Corinthians 12:9

THE WHISPER I LONGED TO HEAR

It all began with a phone call that would drastically change my life as I knew it. I arrived home from church on a warm afternoon in late September, and the phone rang. The voice on the other end was that of a woman I did not know. She identified herself as a doctor from Lakeland Regional Hospital in Florida. Her voice began to waiver as she gave the reason for the call. She informed me that my husband, Herman, was in critical condition in ICU and they weren't sure if he'd survive. He had had a hemorrhagic stroke, which has a low survival rate. All I could do was just sit and listen in disbelief.

My husband was in Florida preaching over the weekend and he was due home Monday. Unfortunately, I was unable to be with him for this trip. As I tried to gather my thoughts to make plans to go to him, I breathed out a prayer. Herman's stroke meant many phone calls, and by this time of day, there were no more outbound flights from upstate New York to Orlando, Florida, which had the closest airport. Booking a flight was difficult because the weather had been problematic for two days, causing endless cancellations and delays all up and down the East Coast.

Finally, I arrived in Florida, not knowing what to expect. Two of our friends picked me up at the airport to take me to my husband. They were doing their best to comfort and encourage me.

During the nearly 60 mile trip to the hospital, they explained to me that he was right in the middle of preaching out of Psalm 86 when the stroke occurred. Once at the hospital, I was struggling to prepare myself for all the sights and sounds of the tubes and machines hooked up to my husband but I was relieved and thankful to finally be there with him.

The next two days were spent meeting with doctors. On the second day, my husband suffered another stroke. Doctors truly doubted his survival at this point and said so. Due to the second stroke, I now found myself sitting with his doctor going over two sets of MRI's. Though I have no schooling in reading MRI's, one look at them showed it went from bad to worse. While waiting for our daughter, Liz, to arrive from Ft. Lauderdale, I spent time in prayer and reading the Bible particularly out of the Book of Psalms. I began to read Psalm 118 and got to verse 17. I just stopped at that verse as it leaped off the page at me, with God whispering His peace to me.

From that point forward I knew my husband would live as it states: "I shall not die but live to declare the works of the

Lord." Our daughter finally arrived, and it was such a comfort to have her there. Our sons could not come at that time and one was deployed in Iraq. However as each day passed, I continued to feel the Lord's peace and saw Herman improve, much to the surprise of the doctors.

One by one tubes that ensured his survival were being removed. I longed to hear his voice and now the tube that had been down his throat was gone, he was able to speak. That ability was completely intact for which I was so thankful to the Lord. His first words to me, in a very raspy voice, barely above a whisper were, "I love you." I bent over to kiss him and a tear rolled down my cheek as I said, "I love you too."

Upon seeing Herman's improvement, his doctor began to ask questions about the peace he saw in me. I told him that it was the peace that passes all understanding and shared with him about knowing the Lord personally. He then said he had seen this same kind of peace in certain hospital volunteers. He stated how he understood that what I had and what they had was even more important than all the medical knowledge he could utilize.

Finally, after eleven days in ICU Herman had improved enough to be transferred to another unit. Though he still had a very long way to go, the words "going home" were like the whisper I longed to hear. At that point, I was told upon discharge he would need placement in a stroke rehabilitation center. That meant I would have to make a trip back to upstate New York to make those arrangements. I hated to leave even for just a few days, but I knew it was necessary as it was one step closer to getting home.

Back in New York finding those arrangements looked impossible. That would be the first half of the battle in getting my husband home. I was willing to look at facilities as far away as Buffalo (which was one hundred miles from our home) in order to find the right placement. Several calls produced no results, but I just kept going down the list I had believing the Lord would help me find that spot. I was given tours of nearby facilities with the understanding that if an opening occurred I would be first on the list to be notified. It was very discouraging but I knew I could not give up.

I was getting to the last facility on the list which was also nearby, when dear friends of ours told me not to bother calling that one because they had personal knowledge that their waiting list was "a mile long." Yet I knew the worst thing they could say was "No beds available." and there was no harm in asking. So I went to the facility to speak to the director. She listened closely to all I had to say and politely said, "We have no beds available but would you like to tour the rehab wing anyway?" I said, "Yes." I was introduced to the head nursing supervisor, who as it turned out, I knew from when I worked in the office of a homecare agency a few years prior. We gave each other a warm hug.

After she heard the details from the director, she stated, "We will have a bed open." The shocked director then turned to me, and as required, asked me for the date of arrival. I said a quick, silent prayer, took a deep breath and gave her a date even though I had no way to get my husband home. Doctors said air travel was too dangerous for Herman and ground transportation was in the multiple thousands of dollars and our insurance would not cover it. I gave them a date anyway knowing they could not hold the bed if we did not arrive by then. Yet within me I was confident that the Lord would not leave us stranded in Florida.

The second half of the battle was waiting for me in Florida. When I arrived, the hospital social worker reiterated the discharge date and handed me a stack of transport companies that would take us the 1,250 miles back to New York. Even the lowest priced one was way beyond our reach. All I could do was find a quiet place to pray which turned out to be the deserted hospital cafeteria patio.

As I poured my heart out to the Lord I looked up to see a tiny rainbow inside of a cloud. In that moment, I was flooded with peace knowing everything was going to be alright. I started back up to Herman's room and just when I stepped off the elevator my phone rang, and the caller was our Bishop. She was checking in on us and wanted to know if we were home yet. Upon hearing what was involved, she said that she would call me back.

Two hours later, she called to say, "You are going home! We took up a love offering to cover the entire cost. Everything has been confirmed with the transport company for you to leave tomorrow." Being overwhelmed, I gasped and thanked her, but I could not contain my tears. The words "going home" that were only a whisper before were now firmly re-sounding in my ears.

After a 26 hour trek back to New York, we finally arrived at the rehab center on the very date I had given them. That was just one of many things shown to me of God's goodness. Once Herman got settled in, I went home, fell on our bed, and just cried. I released everything that had been held in-side and thanked the Lord that we were finally home. After six months at rehab, Herman would really be home too.

We've had many challenges since that day in September 2009. In caring for my husband, who needs 24/7 supervi-sion, there have been ups and downs, frustrations, times of exhaustion and times of tears. Yet there have also been times of joy and laughter and a deep, quiet appreciation for the little things, like my husband being able to read. I could not walk through any of this by myself. None of it has been easy and many times still isn't. It has been a journey of persever-ing against great odds. Through it all, the Lord's peace that passes all understanding, has sustained me. I have found His grace to be sufficient for me and His strength has shown it-self most effectively in my weakness. All along the way, His joy has been my strength.

We can take nothing in this life for granted, especially our loved ones because we are not promised tomorrow. We are all just one phone call away from having our lives change drastically. When you find yourself in the middle of life's challenges and feeling very much alone, I want you to know that there is One Who loves you and cares for you. He does hear your cries for help. That One is our Creator, the Lord Jesus Christ. He never intended for any of us to do life alone. He longs to have a personal relationship with each of us. That begins by us receiving forgiveness from Him. He gives us a new life when we surrender to Him. The Lord promises He will never leave us or forsake us for His name is Emmanuel: God with us. So when you find the journey too hard and the road too long, come to Him and give Him your heart and all your broken pieces. He will walk with you even through the darkest valley. He has taken my story to make it "His-story", a work of His grace to leave a legacy for others to see that He gives peace in His presence and joy for the journey.

About the Author

Sandra Cruz and her husband live in Virginia and have four grown children. As evangelists, they have both shared the hope of the Gospel message in jails, prisons, rehab programs, churches as well as on an individual basis in over 45 years of ministry.

Chapter 5 – Arielle Devito

Ecclesiastes 3:11-13 NLT

11 *Yet God has made everything beautiful for its own time. He has planted eternity in the human heart, but even so, people cannot see the whole scope of God's work from beginning to end.* **12** *So I concluded there is nothing better than to be happy and enjoy ourselves as long as we can.* **13** *And people should eat and drink and enjoy the fruits of their labor, for these are gifts from God.*

BE MORE THAN FIT

Are you "built differently?" Come to find out, I am. Actually, I've known it all along, but I had to go through a lot of "trial and error" to be reminded of who I was created to be, and that my worth is so much more than a number on a scale.

Exercise, defined in this context as working out or regular physical activity, has brought me through so many difficult chapters of my life. In each chapter, exercise prepared me to find my worth outside of obtaining a six pack, a thigh gap or a tight butt. My hope is that as you read my story, you will consider how exercise could be your next step in improving your quality of life. Whether you're a beginner or starting over again, your life can improve more than you might imagine.

We all have an inner desire that longs to be filled, and we set goals to achieve what we can see, feel, touch, and experience. Unfortunately, often we are only temporarily satisfied and learn that it wasn't all we thought it was going to be. For me, I believed being successful looked and felt like going to college, getting a degree, obtaining a well paying, long term career, getting married, having kids, a banging bod and a nice home. Yes, in that order, and yes, teaching my kids to follow the same path. I fully bought into that belief and felt like a failure as my life didn't look like that at all. That belief became the launchpad from where I measured my self worth and the standard that I had to dismantle in order to redefine what success meant for my life.

Chapter 1: Growing Up

I grew up in the church of the Nazarene, as a Christian, committing my life to following Christ when I was eleven. I remember the opportunity to accept Christ as my savior, in the car with my mom, in the Ames parking lot. My grandfather was a pastor. My grandmother played hymns on the piano, and my parents became the youth group leaders at the church we attended. I had been taught that sex before marriage was sinful and therefore, I had a personal conviction about waiting for marriage, so I could do it "the right way." The way I had been taught.

I had focused on boyfriends since seventh grade because it seemed to fill the hole in my heart from what was left when my friends shifted into new friend groups back in sixth grade. The friends I had all through elementary school seemed to be disappearing by "cliquing up" with each other and I felt alone. I felt ditched. I didn't "clique" and by my own observations, I wasn't gorgeous or fit into the molds that the other girls were fitting into. So, when I found out that a boy liked me and wanted to hang out sometime, I agreed. That became the black hole that sucked me into not having any good friends outside of my romantic relationships. Don't get me wrong, having a boyfriend can be great. But for me, my loyalty to and desire to hang out with my boyfriend took me away from any possible new friendship. I had become pretty comfortable with the title and responsibilities of being a girlfriend and long-term relationships became my norm. If the love is good, then I'm in it for the long haul. I do pride myself on loyalty.

One day in eighth grade, at the end of English class while my friends and I waited for the bell to ring, the conversation of sex came up. It was the first time that I was confident enough to utter the words, "Yeah I'm not gonna have sex. Knowing my luck, I'd end up pregnant!" I so badly wish my 13 year old self had realized the power of those words. Those words, plus sex without birth control, equal results I was well aware of, but not in any way prepared for.

Tenth grade came, and I started to realize that I had spent so much time with boyfriends and not with girl friends that I was missing out on the memories that I saw others creating. My romantic relationships weren't bad, I was just tired of being in one. I broke it off, I ended the relationship I had been in since my freshman year, and I felt free. Free to have choices, free to be me, to be single, to just be.

Chapter 2: High School

I want to invite you to be sixteen again and see this story through teenage eyes. You go to my high school and know me pretty well. The things we do (you know, the ones that we shouldn't) tend to "fly under the radar" of our parents, at least to our knowledge. I'm a good kid, and my parents trust me. I follow most of their parental expectations, so there's no need to worry about getting caught.... As long as we hang at your house and not at mine!

Keeping the peace at home means cleaning like I had been asked, being home by a certain time, and always calling to let my parents know where I'm going to be. If "normal teen stuff"; going to parties, occasionally smoking pot and having sex with my boyfriend, also follows those rules, we're good! Look, we both know that this level of "being bad" doesn't compare to what other people are doing so we're okay. As long as I don't push the envelope too far, we can have fun and stay safe. Rebellious, but not too rebellious. "Responsibly irresponsible."

Along Came Aaron

And then, Aaron happened. I had a crush on this guy since 8th grade... He was hot and by my standards, "out of my league." My crush just happened to be on the stage crew with me for the high school musical. One of the cast members came up to me, "Hey. Can you ask Aaron if he'll go out with me?" This was my chance to talk to him! I had an actual reason to approach him! So I asked, my nerves were jittery but I went bravely, hoping his response would be no. He said, "I'm not really interested..." and that was the open door! The butterflies, the "holy balls, I just talked to Aaron!"

There's a cast party after the show, and since I had a new level of confidence, I asked him if he wanted to go with me. He agreed, and it went well. On the way home to drop him off, I placed his hat on my head and pretended to fall asleep, "unintentionally" drooping my head so it landed on his shoulder. Lame, but so fulfilling. It made history!

A couple of weeks later, at a final exam's study session/sleepover at my friend's house, one of my friends on the cheerleading team called him (once she found out I liked him) and asked if he'd consider dating me. Guess what happened? I just scored the hot boy of my middle school dreams! Once word got out, all the girls who heard who I was dating confirmed it for me. "Oh, you're dating Aaron?! He's so hot!" Yeah, I know!

Our junior year was heaven. We never fought about anything, we laughed, we watched cartoons together and drank strawberry milk in 24 oz glasses. The whole thing was EPIC. For the first time ever, I had no intentions of a long-term relationship. I just wanted to have fun. Junior prom solidified my falling in love with this guy. He danced and made a fool of himself and didn't care what anyone else thought. He was just a blast to be around.

We started our senior year together. In November 2002, I got nauseous during cheer practice. A missed period and pregnancy test later, our fears were confirmed. I got bigger, and our friends got scarcer. We attended our senior ball, our chem-free grad party, and walked the graduation stage with

"Tommy, in the tummy." Did it surprise me that I graduated eight months pregnant? Nope. Not one bit. Do you remember what I said back in eighth grade? Those words, plus sex without birth control, equaled results that would forever change our post-graduation plans. Yeah, your words matter!

Side note: every time I come back to this scenario, it makes me laugh a little because what you speak and think, you will attract into your life. I laugh because my mother will say, "having sex is what made you pregnant, not saying you'd get pregnant!" And while that's one hundred percent true, I believe it is also one hundred percent true that what you're speaking over your life is not only what you attract, but also a sign of things to come. And good or bad, you better be preparing for it to show up!

Chapter 3: A Good Thing Gone Wrong

Maybe you're asking yourself, " What does exercise have to do with all of this?" We're getting there! Aaron and I decided to stay together and raise a baby. It's the right thing to do, and we're going to stand by our choices. But as I'm sure you know, the right thing to do isn't always the easiest thing to do. Aaron and I found ourselves in the middle of resentment because he gave up his dreams to take advantage of an out of state college scholarship and instead attend a local community college and work full time.

I found myself lonely, raising a baby in my mother-in-law's house, while I watched everyone else chase the same dreams that I had for myself. Unresolved hurts and arguments lead to emotional abuse and then physical abuse. We would have fights in the car, fights in the house, and yelling matches that cut my self worth and confidence to nothing.

We got married at twenty and welcomed Dominic the year that we turned twenty one. The age you feel officially an adult, like you can actually go out and make something of yourself. Except I didn't. I didn't want friends, I didn't want to go out, I was emotionally and physically exhausted and had gained 40 pounds from my second pregnancy. My self worth was non-existent. We were on the verge of divorce and there were suspicions of my husband at least being emotionally attracted to another woman at his job. My loyalty to this relationship and to my kids was wearing me down, and I couldn't find a way to rise above the situation.

Dom turned one, and I had a conversation with a coworker that reminded me that I had a choice. I could either stay in my misery, or I could do something about my lack of confidence. I knew I couldn't change him, but I could work on myself. If I was going to stay in this to "fight the good fight", I was going to need to pull up my big-girl pants and do something to save me. A flier for group fitness classes came across our desk at work, and I signed up. Cardio kickboxing might be fun, and I could use whatever fun I could get. In truth, this is where it all came together, even though I couldn't see it right then.

I hope you see that there's always a paradox present. A paradox is, "a seemingly absurd or self-contradictory statement or proposition that when investigated or explained may prove to be well founded or true." I want to be sure that you understand this fully because as you reflect on what you've gone through in your life, you'll see that the struggles you've faced end up serving you in the end.

Country Music Launch

Sherri taught the group fitness classes; a non-judgmental, smiley woman who would walk around the room teaching the class like she was genuinely happy that you came. She watched me start in the back of the room, alone. She watched me move up a row each semester until I was two rows from the front. My confidence and consistency had grown, my extra weight and insecurity had left. When I had to defend myself in a fight, I felt like I could stand my ground. It didn't make arguing or fighting any less traumatic, but it did help me feel like I could withstand it if it wasn't going to stop.

One day, Sherri announced that her husband had landed a record deal as a country music singer, and she needed someone to take over teaching the classes. Coincidentally, at the same time, I was getting curious about becoming a Certified Personal Trainer. The timing was magic. She taught another class member and me how to teach group fitness classes and encouraged me to become a personal trainer.

Chapter 4: The Turn-around

Since then, I have started personal training services and group fitness classes at four different fitness centers. I opened my own brick and mortar fitness studio, creating a team of amazing trainers and instructors. I continue to work with coaching clients who want to improve the quality of their lives. Aaron and I named my business "Be More Than Fit", which is exactly what it's helped me become. When you change your mind about what's possible, you can simultaneously improve your mental health and physical health. I never expected the best results of exercising would be found in the way it rebuilt so much of my character. I'm also thrilled to tell you that my husband and I have moved onto a new chapter of our relationship, which is abuse-free because we committed to changing our minds about what was possible for us.

In A Nutshell

I've achieved being the strongest, leanest, healthiest level that I've ever been. Being strong and thin did NOT improve my self worth. I've been the biggest, most unhealthy version of myself too and guess what? Not being on a diet or having extra weight did NOT define my worth either. I've told myself that being thinner or stronger would make me feel better about myself. I've bought into the lie that when we're as good as the person we admire most that we'll finally be successful.

The day I met the woman who I admired so much in the fitness industry made me realize the exact opposite is true. I will never look like her, no matter how many push-ups or squats I am able to do. No matter how perfect my diet is, she had a smaller frame than I had and had a different body type. Even though I had followed her fitness plans for years, I would never look like her. That didn't disqualify me from being able to chase my goals. No matter what I accomplish, my worth lies in who I am, not what my body looks like.

The truth is we're only as worthy or successful as the words we speak, the thoughts we think, and the action we take right now. In this very moment, you have a choice to make. Will you stay in your current state of confidence? How long will you stay loyal to something that isn't helping you improve the quality of your life?

Hindsight is 20/20, which means that you can't see the future clearly. When you look back, you can see EVERYTHING crystal clear. YOUR WORDS MATTER. What you say about yourself, what you think about yourself, what you say to others matters. Girl, listen. You can have whatever life you want regardless of what you've gone through. You can have whatever life you want without comparison to the women you think look better or are more successful than you.

What you speak over your life, how you show up for yourself, and how you show up for others will determine the trajectory of your path. Don't wait another minute. Decide that you're worth doing something for NOW. One step into a fitness class, onto the pavement, or into the gym might be the best thing you'll ever do. You might just find out that you're "built differently" for a reason.

About the Author

Arielle DeVito lives in Knoxville, Tennessee with her husband, two of their three boys, two dogs, and a cat. In her spare time, she enjoys catching up with friends and a good family game night. She loves finding creative ways to live healthfully and inspiring others to do the same. You can connect with her on her social media pages and find out more about how you can "Be More Than Fit" on her business website:

Chapter 6 – Catherine Landschoot

Delight yourself in the LORD,
and he will give you the desires of your heart.
Psalm 37:4

WHY NOT?

My parents were high school sweethearts who married on Valentine's Day with hearts and heads filled with expectations promoted in the pages of fairy tales. Their storybook dream of marriage, family, and a white-picket fence had begun. Mom was 13 and dad 15 when they met. As soon as mom graduated high school they completed chapter one with "I do", and quickly became ready for chapter two.

Overjoyed to announce the pending arrival of their first child, they began their journey into parenthood. Little flutters of life only mom could feel became palpable movements dad could share. As the first trimester moved into the second, conversations turned from "What time will you be home from work today?" and "What's for supper?" into "Who do you think she'll look like?" and "What do you think he'll be when he grows up?"

Mom's trip-to-the-hospital bag had not yet been packed the day they went in.

Miscarriage is never easy but surely the devastation of it grows in alignment with the length of the pregnancy.

Rainbow babies are beautiful, healing bundles of blessing. They replenish shattered hearts and restore hope. The doctors had offered encouragement that they should try again, and although a strong measure of fear had been added to the recipe, they found new joy when she became pregnant again. Around her sixth month, the nightmare repeated itself. There was no rainbow, only black clouds and showers of tears that would repeat again, and again, and again...

How do we find shelter in such storms? What kind of umbrella can possibly cover the showering of such tears? They lost seven babies before mom was finally able to carry a full-term pregnancy. The elusive rainbow finally broke through the darkness with number eight. My existence on this planet was made manifest in the depths of darkness and disappointment. At long last, the clouds parted and the spell had been broken! The cocktail of tenacity, apprehension, relief, gratitude, and joy had to have been intoxicating as they returned home with a living, breathing child in their arms.

As they crossed the threshold of the final weeks of her second successful pregnancy we worked on the finishing touches of preparation. My little two-year-old self was growing and mom's lap was shrinking as we readied for the addition to our family. Little animals pranced across the wallpaper of the new baby's room. Downy-scented clouds of steam rose out of the cloth diapers as the iron hissed across them. The softness of mom's big belly pressed against me as she reached over to help me match the corners of the warm fabric as we folded them and added to the stack growing out of the narrow end of the wooden ironing board above my head.

I was safely tucked away when they headed to the hospital. Mom was whisked to the maternity ward and dad took his seat in the waiting room, in the tradition of the times. He waited... for hours... "Your wife nearly died", they told him, "but she's going to be okay". They went on to explain that his baby boy had lived for only a couple of hours before passing. They were sorry, and they had made all of the necessary arrangements. Neither of my parents ever laid eyes or hands on him. There was no ultrasound, no pictures.

Several days later, they buried a tiny closed casket in the family cemetery plot amidst tears and grief I can only imagine and do not recall. What I know is my baby brother never came home.

We don't choose who is born into our lives, but to adopt? That's different! I was five and Christopher was three on that bright, sunny day. Hungry ducks splashed about in the water, anxiously awaiting the broken pieces of bread I would share with my new brother to quiet their quacking. I barely made it through introductions before reaching for his hand in anticipation of our trip down the winding pathway to the water. As I reached out to take his hand, he abruptly pulled it away, swinging his arm behind him and out of my reach.

Undaunted, I begged him on, trying to tempt him with the bread bag. After a nudge from the adoption agent he finally followed along. Happily, the two of us fed those ducks a fine feast. Sadly, it was the first of many times to come that he would pull away.

My brother was so very wanted and loved. Our parents worked diligently to provide stability and support. He and I developed a strong bond over the years, but the same resistance that drew his hand away from me remained.

The strain was between him and mom. Over the years, his resistance grew into outright defiance. There were times he would literally stare her down and refuse anything she asked of him. I remember the time a simple request to pass the jelly at the breakfast table broke into a catastrophe that dad and I still refer to as "the grape jam incident". Mom's persistence coupled with Chris's resistance blended into a nasty recipe, driven by deep-rooted beliefs neither were willing or able to compromise; beliefs born in disappointment.

He and I would often talk after "incidents". The first big, "why" in my life was incited by his attitude. I wanted to know what made him so angry and belligerent with her. There was never a clear-cut answer. I honestly don't think even he really knew. What I know now that I didn't know then is that our experiences of approaching, engaging, and completing the adoption process had been vastly different from one another. While I had been full of excitement and joy over gaining a little brother, he had been filled with fear and dread over losing his family.

My understanding deepened upon discovery that his foster family had wanted to adopt him but were unable. In their bitterness they apparently told Chris things like, "the new family is taking you away from us". "They are going to be mean to you", and "they're going to make you do things you don't want to do". What a burden to place on a three-year old child! How sad that we can be so self-centered and cruel in the face of grief. His foster family had every right to feel pain in their loss, but how we handle our pain has a ripple effect. The longevity of unhealthy thinking can be lifelong; and for my brother, it was.

With the exception of our parents, we were the only constants in each other's lives. We moved back and forth across the country, then outside the country altogether. We continued to move about even after returning to the U.S. Every move resulted in loss of family, friends, and familiarity. Lots of life lessons, and lots of disappointment. I didn't care so much for the leaving but arriving always felt like a new adventure for me. He didn't care for any of it.

Talk about "making you do things you don't want to do!" By the time I graduated high school we had lived in 13 different houses and attended 10 different schools.

I found my escape in the fall of the year I graduated and married my high school sweetheart. We were 18 and 19 and, contrary to the doubts and speculation of many, it wasn't because we "had" to. We wanted a family for sure! We would banter back and forth about whether we should have an odd or even number of children. I had undergone surgery two years earlier to remove a 7-lb ovarian cyst as well as my left ovary. We were unsure whether or not we would be able to have kids at all, but we hoped.

After we were married my parents came clean about some of the details they had spared me from during that time in my life. They recalled how the doctors had informed them how dangerous my condition was and that the cyst was so large, if I had taken a hit of any kind by any of my soccer teammates or opponents, it would have burst, and I would not have survived.

They continued to explain the initial diagnosis of cancer and recommendations that I begin chemotherapy immediately. They had requested a second opinion and activated a multi-national prayer chain that preceded said opinion which resulted in a clean bill of health with no further action necessary. What a mighty God we serve!

Our quest for parenthood began with a miscarriage just a few weeks into my first pregnancy. How in the name of all things good and holy had my parents persevered in their plight? I felt jabs of emptiness every time I saw a pregnant belly, which seemed to show up everywhere I looked. The whole scenario set into motion my second big "why?", which strangely unrelated to not getting pregnant, was why had I been the only survivor out of all those babies my parents lost.

Over the course of ten years, we made five more babies. God chose to allow us to have and to hold four; two girls and two boys. They were (and still are) the most beautiful and amazing humans ever born! We were so very grateful for every one of them and for the family we were building. I became more and more aware of how blessed we were and so proud of my kids. At the same time I became more and more aware of how many kids didn't have what we had. I became absolutely driven to share our blessings with as many as I was able to.

I became involved in youth ministry at the small Nazarene Church we called home. I spent tremendous amounts of time and energy sharing our family with kids whose lives were not like ours. I wanted the love we shared to impact them and give them experiences that would strengthen them. I believed that, just maybe, we could offer them some of what might be missing from their lives. I hoped the love we shared with them would impact their families, and they would grow to know, love, and serve a God who will never let them down.

We grew a tiny little Sunday School class into a youth group that was attended by more than 100 students over the course of 4 years. I saw God's hand move and felt his presence in ways I had never experienced before. I prayed for my kids, every one of them, daily. I prayed they would feel God's presence and find His purpose in their lives. Never in my worst nightmares did I ever picture the tremendous loss and pain lurking just around the corner.

Sometimes we lose sight of what is right in front of us and, instead, focus on what we hope will be. I did some damage within my own family, not seeing everything from their perspective. I hadn't realized that the day I came home from a Youth Worker's Seminar and announced to my husband that God had called me to youth ministry and "Nothing is going to stand in my way", he heard, "I don't care what you think, this is what I'm doing". I hadn't realized that my children felt like they weren't as important as my "other" kids. They didn't realize they were the very reasons I wanted to reach out. I stepped down from my position when I saw the shadow side of what I was doing.

Then the real nightmare began and my third "why?". "Why them?" Time passed, and my "other" kids started dying; both spiritually and literally.

The spectrum of loss stretched from simply walking away from the church, to incarceration, addiction, drug overdose, and suicide. These were not the outcomes of the "promises" I had diligently stood upon. I was shaken to the core of my being. I was so angry with God! I did everything I could to convince myself that the whole "God" thing was the fairy tale - and I wanted to know WHY? I was done with it all, but God didn't let go.

Psalm 37:4 says, "Take delight in the LORD, and he will give you the desires of your heart." (NIV) Seeking God's will rather than my own allows me to focus on a bigger picture; trusting that he knows my heart's true desires even better than I do. When I find my delight - my strength, happiness, and direction in Him, I don't get what I thought I wanted.

He gives me more than I was even willing to ask Him for. He knows more than I know, so he knows what would make me happier than I can even consider! That's so amazing!

How empowering to know that we get to choose what to feed! As I work to see my trials as opportunities to grow, disappointments lose their strangling holds, pain lessens, and my sense of purpose strengthens. The same "peace that passeth understanding" that was demonstrated by my parents plays itself out in my own life.

We create our lives in direct correlation to the beliefs we hold. Our beliefs drive our actions and our actions result in (natural) outcomes. While we can't control what happens to us, we do have the ability to control how we respond. How absolutely imperative it is that we come to the point in our lives that we are willing to learn this truth. When I think I can, I will, at the very least, make an attempt. When I think I can't, I won't even consider it as an option. Oh, be careful little thoughts what you think!

Unreasonable expectation is the lifeblood of disappointment just as acceptance is the lifeblood of growth. One doesn't happen without the other. Sadness and sorrow are emotions and emotions are temporary. We work through our emotions and find ways to carry on. Grief is not the same as sadness. Grief is a state of being that forms when something happens that we didn't "expect"; unreasonable expectation. My shoulds and shouldn'ts are not reasonable expectations. They are reflections of my own (selfish) desires.

When I don't get what I want, I'm apt to pitch a fit. Thoughts can jump into our minds like fleas on the back of a dog. Media bombards us with ridiculous and unattainable ideas about what we "need", as if happiness can be bought and owned. We become convinced that life should be comfortable, pain in any form can be medicated away, and the world owes us a living. The thoughts we indulge grow from microscopic amoebas into massive and immovable mountains. We can't control what pops into our heads, but our thoughts cannot grow without being fed. Those we feed with fear will lead to darkness and death. Those we nourish with faith will lead to light and life.

One of my strongest coping mechanisms is to avoid remembering dates. I guess, I would rather concentrate on the time we had together than on when someone I love died. So, minus much in the way of detail, I will share that intermingled with all I've just spoken about, my husband's oldest brother died at the ripe old age of 43 due to complications of diabetes. Mom died of cancer at 61. My brother, who was the epitome of physical fitness, died of cancer when his only child was just 10 years old. Several years later my beautiful marathon-running sister-in-law, Charlene, died of a stroke and my incredible nephew, Curran, was left without either of his parents. I do my best to follow Curran on Facebook, but the thoughts implanted by his foster family spilled into Chris's life, creating distance that still exists.

When I consider the losses I have experienced in my life, I now realize it is not loss in and of itself, but rather my unmet expectations that cause my feelings of sorrow, fear, anger, and hurt. It is not our losses, but our disappointments that result in grief that we cannot let go. I'll be honest, I have never laid awake in bed dreaming that one day, if things go right, I'll be disappointed! None of us desire it, but neither do we escape it. However, if we will just step out far enough to listen, God has an answer waiting for us.

While dust and disappointment have lined the path I have traveled all my life, I have learned that how I allow myself to experience my disappointments determines whether the dust clouds my vision or settles beneath my feet. God tells us to "Consider it pure joy, my brothers and sisters, whenever you face trials of many kinds, because you know that the testing of your faith produces perseverance." James 1:2-4 (NIV)

Now I know, there is joy in the journey. No longer do I ask "why". Instead, I ask, "why not?" God's grace is sufficient for me.

About The Author

Catherine Landschoot is a wife of 40 years, mom of four, and Mimi to seven! She spent the better part of the last 20 years working with incarcerated individuals in County and State facilities in the great State of New York as an Addictions Counselor. Having founded Make It Matter Ministries in 2020, Catherine now specializes in grief coaching, providing individual, family, and group life coaching services, and is available for speaking engagements. Check out www.makeit-matterministries.org for more information.

Chapter 7 – Jessica Roman

Release the pressure to perform perfectly. You are enough as you are, creating greatness in your natural abilities.

THE CAPE OF CREATIVITY IS YOUR SUPERPOWER

My story began in the summer of 1982, when I was born to teenage parents who met over Brooklyn pizza. New York, that is, where everyone walks or catches a bus. My mother, as fly as she is, always kept her make-up flawless. And on a random weekday afternoon, she walked into a pizzeria where my dad was working. They shared smiles. And almost a year later, they shared a child. Welcome to the world, Jessica Marie Roman.

Over the next few years came three more children, a marriage, and responsibility. As the oldest of four, I was my mother's right hand. Being of Puerto Rican descent, we spent a lot of time in the kitchen. Some of my favorite memories with my mom came from listening to her sing oldies tunes on the radio station while whipping up the groceries. Spirited and spunky, she was my muse.

Some of our favorite meals included rice and peas (arroz con gandules), roast pork (pernil), and empanadas (meat patties). Of course, mom balanced the meals with salad and vegetables.

However, I would often bury them under the rice. Even back then, I thought outside of the box.

You may even argue that burying the mushy green peas and carrots was borderline manipulative. Honestly, I can't remember if my intent was good or bad, but I knew I didn't want to eat them. I also knew that I didn't want to get the lecture on kids starving in third-world countries and how we needed to be grateful for the food on our plates.

My parents were tough on me because they wanted better for my siblings and me than they had for themselves. After all, it's a hard knock-life living in the inner city. We often heard police sirens blaring every hour of the night, arguments from the neighbors living above or below us in the project buildings, and every now and then a random shootout that sought us seeking shelter.

IN OUR OWN HOMES. You heard that right. We had a shoot-out plan, much like a fire escape plan. We all knew that if we heard random gunshots to find cover under the kitchen table or in the bathroom tub - whichever room was closest.

My parents wanted better opportunities for their children. Mom, in her soothing voice, often spoke words of encouragement and life into me. Tranced by her low and soft tone, her exact words would slip my mind. However, I knew her voice and that it put me at ease. My father was a man of few words and set the example for what consistency and hard work looks like. It was their actions and words that helped me believe that I could be anything I wanted to be. However, this wasn't without a few challenges.

As a free-spirited thinker, guided primarily by emotions, I often found it hard to focus on one thing. If you feel this way, you also may be a creative thinker. Our imaginations take over and

We come up with the most brilliant ideas. However, if you are like me, we can get lost in our imagination and struggle with taking action. Allow me to take you back to my earliest memory of struggling with feelings of being overwhelmed, discouraged, and unsure.

I was in sixth grade. A well-mannered, curvy, smart girl with braces. Our science project assignment that year was to create the components of a cell. As the teachers proudly showed pictures of the winners of last year's science fair, I was inspired. The winners went ALL OUT, decorating huge styrofoam balls with fancy spray paints, vibrant play doughs, and 3D floral wires. As the winners proudly held their trophies, I couldn't help but notice their goofy smiles. I wanted that feeling, so I went after it.

With three weeks to plan, I wanted my project to be the BEST. At the time, I didn't know there was such a term to describe what I was feeling inside. My parents had validated me as being talented, driven, and gifted with my hands. However, I remember my feelings of perceived inadequacy in that moment. The thought of not having a trophy consumed me. And I went through what some may term today as "Imposter Syndrome." Defined as chronic self-doubt and intellectual fraudulence that may override feelings of success or external proof of one's competence.

For the next few weeks, I experienced anxiety day in and day out. The "All or Nothing" attitude paralyzed me from taking action to do further research on my project. In my mind, I had already been defeated because I didn't think I could create something like what the teachers had shown as previous examples. And then, the night before the science fair, I broke down and spilled the beans to my mom. "Hey mom, I have this science project due tomorrow... do you have any scissors, glue, tape, cardboard paper, styrofoam, etc.?" She nervously laughed and said, "Who do you think I am, Walmart? And whyyyyyy are you telling me this NOW? It's due tomorrow!" With regret, I let out a defeated low groan as I said "Mom, I don't know." Without force, I lowered my head and shed a tear.

As I went into the bathroom to gather myself, a little bit of hope hit me. Surprisingly, I noticed the shape of the soap on the bathroom sink resembled the shape of a cell. I also noticed that the soap could be carved and shaped because it was soft enough to dissolve with a little water. Excited and with new energy, many thoughts raced into my head on how I could carve the cell.

Suddenly, there was hope. And miraculously, in that moment, I cracked a smile.

LIGHTBULB MOMENT!

My science project was going to be carved from a bar of soap and I was going to identify the inner components of the cell with toothpicks and attached sticky notes. This was my creative plan and it worked. Even though I didn't win a trophy, I did receive an "A" on my science project that year. This was the first time I truly felt like one could be successful with an original idea.

As time went on and I became an adult, I developed this confident *city girl swag*. I realized that this traditional work of 9-to-5 was BORING. It's not that I was irresponsible. I had other thoughts of having fun while working. Oftentimes, my mind would drift into hypothetical conversations with myself as I would ask, "Why is it that musicians get to play music for a living, dancers get to sweat and earn at the same time, and why do they get to have all the fun? By the way, is it 4:59pm yet?" UGH.

During these years, I resorted to what my mother introduced me to as a child, playing in the kitchen. Creating in the kitchen was therapy for me. It was my field of study that had no rules, no conditions. With a few ingredients, you could be committed to creating something, anything. Although my mother introduced me to the kitchen at the tender age of seven as her assistant cooking hot savory foods, I found my niche as an adult in the vast world of cake decorating.

Funny story: - I think back on the nights when I stayed up into the wee hours of the morning perfecting my butter-cream piping skills. I would have to wait until everyone went to bed because that's when I had the kitchen all to myself, and it was okay to make a MESS. Ha-ha.

My mother would wake up after a full 8 hours sleep to entire cakes being thrown in the trash. With much passion and surprise, she would scream, "Jessica what is wrong with you??? Why are all of these cakes in the garbage?" I would reply, "Mom because it didn't look right." She replied with a blank stare and an invisible question mark on her forehead. "You threw the cakes away because they didn't LOOK right?!?!?!?!?!" She would just shake her head and walk away. I, however, knew that this was the beginning of a lifetime love story.

From there, I've figured out a few of life's recipes. Let's take a look at the ingredients of cake and the roles they play in the big picture. A standard cake recipe typically includes flour, sugar, eggs, butter or oil, milk or water, a leavening agent, and some type of flavoring. Play along with me as we liken each important step to the recipe of your own life.

First, flour gives the cake its strength and holds ingredients together, thanks to the proteins that mix with water to form gluten. Without flour, the cake would be a runny mess. Ewwwe, who wants a red velvet pudding? Certainly not me! Ironic however, this being the most important ingredient of a cake, is the messiest. I don't know about you, but one of the worst things in life is getting caught in a cloud of flour while making pie crust. It gets everywhere!! However, would you say that the flour in your life was necessary? That the trials and tribulations, your ups and downs have made you strong? If so, you are building your own recipe, your own testimony. The flour is the backbone to your custom tiered cake of life.

Second, butter and oil improve the cake's texture, moistness, and overall flavor. It's the fat that makes it taste so good! So, when you are going through a season when you feel like cake crumbs, don't freak out! There's still value in the cake crumbs, especially if they are extra moist...

Third, you can't skip the eggs! Without the eggs, the other ingredients will not bind together. The eggs in your life are the transition seasons that help you "Level up!" Take the lessons from the previous seasons and put them in perspective. Always strive to become a better version of yourself, not a lesser version of someone else.

Fourth, you need liquid for hydration. Liquid vaporizes during the baking process and creates steam, which expands the volume of the cake. Imagine the smell of a freshly baked banana nut bread with steam coming from the top. It's fresh, hot, and touches your soul on a whole different level. Please welcome the steam in your experiences, it means you still have breath in your body and air in your lungs. It's the steam that keeps your perspective fresh and alive.

Fifth, we need sweetener! After all, it's the reason why we prefer cake over bread, right? How about sweetness on the tongue? How are we speaking to ourselves and the ones around us? It's been said that words hold power and that we manifest what we think, and eventually speak. Speaking all things kindly will not only help you but bless someone else's day in the process. Remember, there is death and life in the power of your tongue. Like honey rolling from our lips, let our words be intentional. Remember, the cake is only a cake because it's sweet!

Lastly, leavening agents, like yeast and baking soda help the cake to rise. When all of the above life ingredients come together, it's time to rise. When situations in life knock us down, we must be intentional with adding the last ingredient. In my opinion, it's the main one. The one that helps us to go higher. The one that creates the most impact. The one that brings all your life's ingredients and seasons into perspective.

For me, building a rewarding and passionate career has been 10 whole years of trial and error, failing forward as some may call it. Not having the money or time for culinary or pastry school,

I've learned the majority of what I know through watching free videos online. After a decade of real-world market research, making thousands of mistakes, and choosing to get back in the game, I now teach virtual culinary courses in a condensed coaching program. Yummy Coaching Factory is half mindset training and half technical training, which is designed for the professional woman seeking to build confidence in the kitchen.

Though the world may not be perfect and it's a mean and nasty place, I want you to know just as equally that there is beauty in the ashes. Good people still exist, great relationships are still possible, and warrior women make things happen. If a city girl like me from the housing projects of East New York can make it, so can you. You must believe in yourself, set your stage, and have the courage to crack your first egg.

About the Author

Jessica Roman is an adventurous woman who appreciates color, theater, and adventure. Faith centered, she and her future husband love nature and spending time on the shores near Tampa, Florida. You can learn more about her zest for life, coaching, and mentoring services at JessicaRomanInspires.com.

Chapter 8 – Tiffany Harris

"When you shift your mindset, there will be a shift in the trajectory of your life!"

A SINNER SAVED

Have you ever witnessed someone being abused and said to yourself, "That would never be me." "I will never be in a relationship with a man that abuses me."

I was raised by both my mother and father, God rest his soul, in a row home in Philadelphia with three sisters and four brothers in a section of the city called Mt. Airy. I remember going to school and talking to my friends about our family. People would say to me, "You are being raised by both your mother and father in the house?" "That must be nice." I used to say to myself, "You think it's nice, but you have no idea." In 1998, my father checked himself into the Veterans Affair (VA) Hospital, and for the first time, was diagnosed with Post Traumatic Stress Disorder (PTSD), Bipolar Disorder, and Depression. The onset of these clinical diagnoses were the result of him being a sniper in Vietnam twice and experiencing a traumatic childhood. However, I wasn't aware of my father's diagnoses, war experience, and childhood trauma until I was 17 years old.

Growing up, I noticed that my father had a temper and seemed to struggle to control his anger. Unfortunately, my mother experienced physical abuse at the hands of my father. One morning, I heard my mother crying and yelling. As I stood in the living room with some of my siblings, I naturally became worried about my mother as her cries got louder. I was scared, but I had to make sure my mother was okay. Shaking and afraid, I slowly walked up the steps leading to the second floor. Before I could get to the top of the steps, I looked to the right and in between the bars of the metal banister I could see the bathroom door open. This heartbreaking view will never leave my memory. Although my mother was sitting in the tub, I could tell she was sitting in the tub against her will. Her legs and feet were up in a defense position as she yelled and begged my father to stop. There my father was, in the tub also, but standing over top of my mother. In his hands was a ladder that was positioned above his head as if he was attempting to hit my mother with it. I can't remember my exact response, but I know it had something to do with me begging my father to stop. During this moment, I can vividly recall saying to myself, "I will never allow a man to abuse me" and that "I wouldn't stay in a relationship with someone who abused me."

In 2005, I was a graduate student at Temple University working on my Master's Degree in Social Work. One day in between classes, I was walking down a very well-known street in Philadelphia called Broad St. I was walking towards Broad and Oxford to be exact. Although the sun was shining, it must have been winter because I can recall seeing him, let's call him Rich, walking towards me with a brown and black fur coat on. We were walking on the same side of the street, but in the opposite direction. As we got closer to walking past each other our eyes locked. Not only did the sun shine, but the sun also shined on his light brown eyes. From his eyes I noticed his beard, then his braids, then his smooth brown skin.

Before I could walk too far past him he spoke. He simply asked me, "How are you?" As I kept walking, I replied, "I'm fine, thank you." He spoke again and asked another question, "Wait, can I talk to you for a second?" I hesitated for a few seconds, then I stopped. He spoke again, "My name is Rich, what's your name?" I was shy and gave a little smile and replied, "Tiffany!" He said, "It's nice to meet you Tiffany, are you headed to work?" I replied by letting him know that I was a student at Temple, and I was headed to get lunch since I was on break in between classes. Rich seemed so caring and thoughtful when he said, "Well, I don't want to take up time from your break so how about we exchange phone numbers so I can take you to lunch one day." On this winter day on Broad St., Rich and I exchanged phone numbers with plans to schedule a date for lunch. I wasn't in a relationship and was actually looking forward to getting to know him more.

As bad as I wanted to call Rich, I waited a few days because I didn't want to appear desperate. So, when he finally called me, I let the phone ring a few times. I didn't pick up right away because I didn't want him to think that I was sitting around waiting for his call. The first time we spoke on the phone I was "cheesing" from ear to ear. Needless to say, as the younger generation would say, I was "hype" to be talking to him on the phone. Rich and I talked on the phone for hours. Some nights we fell asleep on the phone because neither one of us wanted to hang up. Rich and I talked on the phone every single day until we scheduled to hang out in person a week later. During the week of talking on the phone all I could think about was how polite, charming, sweet, and good looking he was.

During the week, I learned that Rich didn't drive so he wanted me to drive to him so we could meet up. He said he would be in the North Philadelphia section of the city. He gave me the exact street and time to meet up. The day had finally come to meet up, and I was so excited. I had to make sure I wore the cutest outfit, including my multicolor fur coat since I remembered that he had on his brown and black fur coat when we first met. Of course, I sprayed my Paris Hilton perfume, which was my favorite perfume back then.

I hopped into my black 2000 Ford Focus, put the address in my GPS, turned my music all the way up, and I was on my way to see Rich. With butterflies in my stomach, I pulled up to the location, but I didn't see him at first. I called his cell phone and he told me that he was in the "Papi Store," which was what all the corner Dominican Stores in Philly were called. I waited, anxiously, for the Papi Store door to open so I could finally hang out with him. The first thing I saw was the same brown and black fur coat. Rich had the hood on this time and his head was down as he walked out of the Papi Store. I started smiling immediately. He walked out of the store with his hood on and slowly raised his head to the point where our eyes locked once again. Now, I got to see him smiling from ear to ear like he was so excited to see me. Me on the other hand, wasn't as excited as I initially was.

He put his hand on the door handle of my Focus, opened the door, and just smiled. Without him saying a word when we locked eyes this time I saw someone different, compared to the person I saw on Broad St that bright and sunny day. This time I saw someone who was a liar, a cheater, a manipulator, and an abuser. However, I thought my eyes and thoughts were playing tricks on me. I literally shook off and disregarded everything I felt and saw. Instead, I said, "Come on, get in" with the same smile on my face and uncertainty in my mind. We were inseparable from the first meet up at the Papi Store. I quickly realized that because Rich didn't have a car that he relied on me to take care of his "business." It turned out that he sold weed. For some women this would be a problem, but for me it was perfect because I smoked weed back then. I went from buying my own weed to dating a man who sold weed. That meant I could get all the weed I wanted for free when I wanted it.

In between going to classes at Temple, I was getting high with Rich every chance I got. Rich and the weed became my main focus instead of my graduate school program. However, a few months into the relationship, I completed my graduate program and earned my Master's Degree in Social Work. Now I didn't have to split my time between Rich and school. It was all about him now. Now that school was over, he seized this perfect opportunity to have me at his beck and call. In retrospect, I realize that I became the driver while he made his drop offs of weed all around the city. However, my addiction was satisfied, so I didn't complain.

One night, I drove Rich into a dark alley in the Northeast section of Philadelphia. He told me to pull up to a house, put the car in park, lock the doors, and he got out of the car. I sat in a dark alley alone, paranoid, and checking my surroundings repeatedly as I waited for him to come back to the car. It may have been 10 minutes, but it seemed like an hour before he came back to the car. I yelled and asked him what took him so long. I told him that I wouldn't be his driver while he rode around selling weed. He knew how to keep me quiet. Just like every other time that I yelled at him, he pulled out a blunt that was already rolled with weed in it. He said, "Here just smoke this." My body craved weed, so as soon as my eyes saw the blunt, I began to smile and was all smiles afterwards. The fact that he had me sitting in a dark alley in an unfamiliar part of the city didn't matter anymore.

I drove Rich to his Aunt's house, which is where he lived. Although he was in his 20's his Aunt was very strict and did not allow him to have females in her house. Therefore, he opened the front door slowly. He and I tiptoed to the basement where he slept. Once we were in the basement he pulled a folded brown package from the front pocket of his hoodie. "Now, what is that?" I whispered since I didn't want to talk too loud because his Aunt might hear. He said, "Bae, you know everything that I do, I do it for us." "Selling this weed is not going to get me enough money to keep getting your car fixed, buying you food, putting gas in your car, buying you stuff, giving you cash, and giving you all the weed to smoke that you want."

Of course, Rich tried to make it seem like this next move was all about me. He placed the brown folded bag on the top of his empty dresser. I waited impatiently as he slowly unfolded the bag. All I could see was something white, but I still wasn't sure what he had. Then he said, "Bae, I'm going to start selling cocaine." Immediately, my high from the weed was blown, and I began to freak out. I became so angry that I had to leave his Aunt's house before she woke up. Rich and I were night owls so we drove around the city arguing about his decision to begin selling cocaine.

As a new graduate from Temple, I wasn't working, and Rich was my only source of income. I was so caught up with all that he was doing for me that I overlooked all of the illegal activities he was involved in, including selling cocaine. At every turn, Rich reminded me that he was the reason that I had new brakes, new tires, food to eat, money in my pocket and all the weed I could smoke. Once again, I had allowed his words to deter me from my better judgment. Things quickly went from me allowing Rich to drive around and sell weed from my Ford Focus to him selling weed and cocaine from my Ford Focus.

Now instead of me being the driver, I allowed him to drive, with no driver's license, while I rode shotgun. I had never been in a relationship with someone like Rich. Although I would ride with him to make his drug deals, I still argued with him about the risks of all that he was doing. He knew that the weed wasn't enough to keep me calm, quiet, and in compliance with his illegal activities. One late night in the middle of me arguing with Rich after he dropped off cocaine to several "regular" customers he said, "Here take this and calm down." I stared at a small bottle that had a pink or purplish color liquid in it. At the bottom of the bottle was a blue pill floating in it and dissolving. He said, "This is called syrup with a Xanax in it." He told me that the concoction was better than weed. I just wanted to stop being upset and relax. The truth of the matter was, although I did all that fussing, I never left Rich.

Blue skies, the moon, blurred vision, and fresh air is all that I saw and could smell when I opened my eyes hours after drinking the concoction Rich had given to me. The feeling I had did not compare to the feeling I had when I just smoked weed. I remember waking up asking, in a low faint voice, "Where are we?" Rich replied, "North Philly." I dozed back off then woke up again and in a low faint voice asking, "Where are we?" he replied, "South Philly." Again, I asked after waking up, "Where are we?" he replied, "In the Northeast." This was the beginning of my addition to now syrup and pills as well as the start of Rich driving my 2000 Ford Focus throughout Philly where he not only sold his drugs, but also stashed his drugs in my glove compartment.

As the number of customers increased, Rich and I were out throughout the night making drop-offs. I got to a point that

I no longer wanted to ride around with him all night, so I gave him approval to drive my vehicle, without me. Up to this point, I had trusted Rich. However, there were nights when he didn't answer my calls. There were nights when he didn't return my calls for hours. I had my suspicions that he was dating someone else, but I didn't have proof at the time. However, I still confronted him, and he was very blunt when he told me that just because no one else would ever want someone who looked like me doesn't mean that he was cheating. This was the first time he had spoken to me in this way. I didn't realize it at the time, but I was in fact being emotionally abused by Rich.

Growing up, there were parts of my body that I never liked, including my big, full lips. So, the more Rich tore down everything about me physically, I internalized it and it affected me mentally. As a result, I suffered from low self-esteem. It didn't matter if I received attention or compliments from others. If it wasn't coming from Rich, I wasn't happy or satisfied with my appearance. It got to the point where I felt like he was doing me a favor by staying with me, because like he said, "Men don't like women who have big lips and no body." He was very specific when he talked about my body. "You have no breast and no butt, so why would a man want you." "You will never get someone like me," Rich would say.

Everything in me knew that Rich was no good for me. It started with selling weed, to selling cocaine, to me drinking syrup and popping pills. Then came the emotional abuse, me being the getaway driver while Rich robbed people at gunpoint, to him cheating on me and daring me to leave him. He even pulled a gun out on me, pulled out my car's spark plugs, slashed my car tires, and put sugar in my gas tank. Then that one thing started to happen that I vowed I would never stand, physical abuse. Although I always said I would never date a man who abused me, here I was in a full blown abusive relationship. That liar, manipulator, cheater, and abuser that I saw the first time he opened my car door wasn't a figment of my imagination. My life was literally spiraling out of control, and enough was enough.

Here I was a college graduate with goals and aspirations that I had no desire to pursue. This was because I made a decision to continue to love and make myself available to a man who abused me emotionally and physically. This man not only pulled a gun out on me and blacked my eye repeatedly, but would also call my cell phone and say, "Oh, you are not dead yet?" I had to have a conversation with myself and ask myself, "What will happen if I don't get out of the toxic relationship?" The answer I told myself was, "Tiffany, you will die." This was the critical, life-saving question and answer that created a shift in my mindset.

I was raised in the church, so I always knew that God was my source of help. I needed God more than ever before. My mother had raised me in church since I was a baby, so not only did I know God, I also knew the power of prayer. One late night after getting high with Rich I dropped him off yet again to his Aunt's house with the expectation that I would be right back early in the morning, so he could use my car to take care of his "business." I had taken enough hits to the face and hidden one too many black eyes. I was done with accepting being one of multiple women because I believed I wasn't good enough. I was tired of trusting in man, Rich, to supply all my needs instead of trusting in God. I was broke and broken, but the toxic life with Rich wasn't the life that God called me to live.

Like I said, Rich and I were night owls so it had to have been almost 2 or 3 am when I rode through the back roads after dropping him off in the Northeast and heading back to my house in Mt. Airy. Although I was high as a kite I began talking to God. I simply said, "God, I need your help. I'm caught up and stuck in this abusive, toxic, and unhealthy relationship, but I don't know how to get out of it." I didn't think that God would really hear me, nor listen to my prayers because I was high on weed, pills, and syrup as I prayed. After praying, I turned the music on to the gospel station, 103.9. The song that was playing as soon as I turned on the radio was, "God still hears a sinner's prayer" by Deitrick Haddon. It is true that God still hears a sinner's prayer. It is also true that, "Late in the midnight hour, God is going to turn it around, and it's going to work in your favor."

"P s l m 9 1," is the license plate that was on the silver motorcycle that sat in front of me at the red light. This was the morning that my stomach was in knots as I drove myself in my 2000 Ford Focus to a court hearing so my Protection From Abuse (PFA) order against Rich could be finalized. Prior to the court date, I cried and literally questioned God after several failed attempts, so I thought, to serve him with my PFA documents. I arrived to the court building that was located in Center City Philadelphia. I was alone, afraid, anxious, and so nervous that I was shaking while on the verge of vomiting. Then I remembered that silver motorcycle that was in front of me at the red light with the license plate, "P s l m 9 1." To me it automatically registered in my mind as Psalm 91.

Peace, tranquility, assurance, and victory describes everything that I felt as I sat in the courtroom, pulled out my pocket Bible, and read the entire Psalm 91 as I waited for my case to be called. Then I was called, Tiffany Gay vs. Rich Wells. Rich was nowhere in sight, so I was the only party that walked into the spacious Judge's chambers decorated with cherrywood furniture. The Judge was polite as he greeted me with a smile and asked me if I had been able to serve Rich the PFA since he wasn't present in court. I explained to the Judge my challenges with serving him, which included the final attempt when Rich scanned the PFA papers and threw them down. Not only did he throw the PFA papers down, he refused to take them. To my surprise, that was enough to consider Rich, "SERVED!" My PFA was in full effect!

After being in this unhealthy, toxic, and near death relationship for almost two years, I regained my self-esteem, peace, and dignity. My faith in God and my relationship with God was restored. For the first time in a long time I felt like I was in control over my life with the freedom to make positive decisions concerning my life. I felt like every chain was broken and every dark cloud that followed me faded away. I was at a place where I had done things my way. However, doing things my way caused my life to be in shambles to a point where I was close to losing my life. It was time to surrender to God. It was time to continue to let go and let God. I thank God for that shift in my mindset, which shifted the trajectory of my life! This life lesson is one that has turned out to be the secret sauce to me thriving in my purpose. As a result of this life lesson I am committed to serving women by empowering them to transform the way their minds are set, so they can live the most rewarding life they were born to live!

To my beautiful and brilliant sister friends, you are enough and you are worthy to be cherished, honored, adored, respected, and loved. You are no one's punching bag or doormat to walk all over. It's true when they say, "warning comes before destruction." Make sure you take heed to the warning signs. Allow my life lesson to be a testament of God's faithfulness and unconditional love that he has for you. I was a sinner that God saved, rescued, healed, and restored. So, I employ you to not allow your past or current circumstance make you think that God will not hear your prayers and answer your prayers. Remember, God still hears a sinner's prayer and late in the midnight hour HE is going to work things out in your favor! I'm a living testimony!

About the Author

Tiffany Harris was born and raised in Philadelphia, Pa. She is a devoted wife and proud mother. Tiffany is an Award Winning International Speaker and the two time award recipient for Change Maker of the Year! She is also the Author of a book titled, From the struggle to the STAGE!nIn addition, Tiffany is a Mindset Coach and Mentor as well as the Founder of an International Women's Community, WIN WOMEN EMPOWER, where women empower women to SCALE, SOAR, and SUCCEED!

To stay connected with Tiffany:
Email: tiffany@tiffanyharris.net
Facebook: Tiffany Harris
Linked In: Tiffany Harris
IG: @Mindsetshiftwithtiff
Scan the QR code to visit Tiffany's website, tiffanyharris.net!

Chapter 9 – Nicky Cuesta

*"Our Deeds are not the basis of our salvation,
they are the evidence of our salvation.
They are not foundation, they are demonstration."*
– John Piper

DEMANDING MY PRESENCE

Life doesn't come with a manual. Have you endlessly sensed being unseen or unheard? Do you continually feel lost in a crowd? Have you felt left in the shadows? Have you avoided the light shining bright on you? Have you let choices from the past define your future? Do you have something to say, but you are never given the chance to speak up? I am here to tell you that you can bounce back from anything to demand your presence.

Unfortunately, I have felt this throughout my teenage years. It began as a young Puerto Rician girl amongst a family with twenty-one cousins. I was born and raised in the Northwest side of Chicago. I was the youngest of two children. My mother's parents had their own version of the Brady bunch. There were three girls and three boys. All, but one of Mom's siblings had two kids each. Ironically, they all had a boy and girl. That made us a total of ten cousins. My grandparents from my biological dad's side had another variation on the Brady bunch, plus two. Four boys and four girls. Making a total of fifteen cousins.

My biological dad and my mom split up when I was only six months old. I didn't have a relationship with him until he came into my life when I was fourteen. It was one of those decisions that I had to ponder. It was hard to accept the fact that he had abandoned us for the most unexplainable reasons. His pride was too large to see that he made a mistake at the time. I was left to make a decision to get his side of the story. After months of rejecting his plea to get to know me, I finally gave him the opportunity to enlighten me. I was still a little skeptical, but eventually, I gave in and took a gamble to get to know him and my family. I am glad that I did.

My mom was left to become a single mother to raise my brother and me when my dad left. After some time, she was introduced to my adopted dad whom she eventually married. When they decided to tie the knot, he was given the opportunity to give us his last name. He didn't have any other children of his own when he married my mom. There was no hesitation to make sure that his last name lived on.

After a few years of trying to make it work. They decided to part ways due to his heavy drinking and never being home. He never went on to remarry or have any other children. He was emotionally, and financially, part of our lives. My brother and I were his children until his last breath. No one could ever tell him that we were not. He didn't care if we didn't share the same DNA. His love for us was undeniable. I will forever carry his name. We lost him in 2004 to liver disease.

After their separation, my mother was alone again for a few years to focus on being a great mother to raise her two prides of joy. After some time, she finally met the man that has kept her heart for thirty-six years. The man that became dad to me at the early age of five. The man that gained the privilege to walk me down the aisle on my wedding day. Our family became blended as we gained five more siblings from his previous marriage, making the average visibility percentage less.

Between cousins and siblings there were a total of twenty-seven of us. So, you can just imagine how hard it could have been for me to stand out. I felt lost in the mix of family gatherings and didn't have the advantages that some of my other family members had.

As years went on, and we started to create our own paths in life, I always felt that I had no clear direction for what I wanted to do or who I wanted to become. I was lost to figure it out all on my own. This led me through some dark times earlier in life. A few seasons of bad choices that I didn't realize were an accumulation of some things that don't make me proud. We usually don't understand these things until years later.

During my elementary years, I was a part of whatever the school had to offer. Dance was my superpower. When the music started, my body just moved to the beat. No matter what genre it was, I would craft an eight count in a heartbeat. I was able to decompress all my emotions through movement. The passion for dance will forever be a part of who I was and for all the days of my life. Eventually things started to change as time moved on. Other interests began to grow stronger.

My interest in sports started about fifth grade all the way through high school. I was the shortest power forward on my basketball team. I loved the game, especially living in the hometown of the famous Chicago Bulls with Michael Jordan winning six championships. I was also a cheerleader for my school's boys' basketball team. I was able to again release anxiety while being part of something bigger than me. I also dabbled in softball too. I enjoyed the team efforts. It was a great experience to travel to away games. It was awesome being a student athlete.

When I got to high school, things started to shift during my freshman year. I was no longer the over achiever. I wasn't interested in being the top of my class. I didn't excel in any vocation. I wasn't in any inner circle. I merely went because I knew I had to. I really didn't love the way I looked. I didn't admire myself. My body type was something I focused on a lot. I felt I was too big. I never interacted with friends outside of school. No hangouts or sleepovers. It was a tough time for me internally. No one ever knew this about me because I was good at suppressing these feelings.

Freshman year, I met my high school sweetheart. All my time before and after school revolved around him. Sometimes even on my weekends, we were together. The relationship was the only highlight of my high school days. I was finally noticed by someone. Someone I could share my time with.

We laughed and we loved each other as we created great memories. We introduced each other to our families shortly after. Every year that passed was another blissful year of possibilities that this would go beyond high school.

During my teenage years I became oblivious to the fact that I had no real knowledge of what I wanted. I was naive to the fact that I wasn't ready for anything serious. Blind love can do that to you. Just like any other young relationship, things started to shift.

For me, it was the summer before going into senior year where the real uncertainty started to manifest. When my character was questioned. Where others became involved in our love story. Where we were tested to the point of having to give each other space because of the choices that we were making. Rethinking if we should continue to make what we thought was magical last a lifetime.

Heading into senior year alone was not how I wanted things to be. It was my final year which included homecoming, senior prom, and graduation. I was totally in a bubble of love for the past three years that I never gave myself the chance to figure out what I wanted to do with my future. I regretted never taking advantage of the experiences that high school offered. Who was I supposed to become? Inevitably, I got back into the same relationship.

Ultimately, I didn't graduate. I gave up in my senior year of high school with just a few months to go. I went straight to work and continued building my relationship. It went on for some time, and we eventually got engaged. Throughout the last year of the relationship things just started to change. Recreational drugs were introduced to the relationship. Marijuana was the primary choice, but it led to cocaine. I didn't see it coming. Most of us never do.

Cocaine is a drug that can really destroy a person, relationships, and life itself. It first started with just trying to stay awake to have a good time. Then it turned into having to have it all the time. The final straw for me was when it interfered with the bond that I thought could never be broken until he became the payment to get high. I was absolutely disgusted with how things ended up. I had to step back and look at what I was putting myself through. I just couldn't believe where I was in life. At this point the relationship was finally over.

As an adult now, I finally had the courage to come out about dating other women. I had always known I possessed these feelings within. I didn't know how to live openly; all I knew was that love is love, and it didn't matter where it came from. I had plenty of time to explore this side of myself throughout the years but chose not to act on it. It happened suddenly when I was reunited with a good friend from high school.

We got to know each other on a deeper level. I had always felt a vibe that something was there but couldn't pinpoint what it was. The attraction got heavier. As we dated for a few months old habits started to resurface. The party life was back in full effect. The drugs got heavier as time went on. I ended up trying acid, ecstasy, and continued with marijuana. At the time, it wasn't a thought. I had someone that was giving me attention, and I was falling hard. So hard that when no one accepted us together in their homes, I would sleep in the streets, in parks and even ride the train back and forth, just so I could be with her. When I thought I had finally freed myself from a self-destructive relationship, it wasn't too long until I noticed I was in yet another toxic association.

I started to really see what my world had come to. I had to do something and I had to do something fast. That was when I made the decision to move to Philadelphia and start fresh. I went with the mindset of finding my true purpose in life. I was ready to write my new chapter. It wasn't easy, but it was the best decision I could ever have made for myself. I started working immediately and eventually met my wife. She was truly the angel that God placed in my life.

When we started dating, she fell in love with the real me. She saw the pain that I still carried. She most importantly saw the heart and grit that I possessed to get my life back in order. She told me about Job Corp. I rocked an eighteen-month Business Technology program in nine months. I became certified in Microsoft Office. I went on to Community College of Philadelphia for Business. Then, I finally got my big break in corporate America at a Health Care Company that believed in me.

When I got the job, I promised myself that I would no longer look back at the past. I would no longer feel ashamed of the choices that I had made. I truly believed that I had to go through the things that I went through to make me the woman I am today. My only agenda from day one at this company was to learn it all and to produce top-quality work. To make my presence known, I made sure I built authentic relationships. I would use pure determination to find my purpose. I was blessed to have found my purpose.

I created many life experiences through my voyage. It was important for me to start a personal development quest. There is no growth if you don't make the necessary changes. I was inspired to build my confidence, to create my own happiness, and to promote positivity no matter where GOD led me. No matter who God led me to, He knew exactly the route that I had to take to get my voice back. I am proud of what I have created for myself along the way. Being able to reinvent myself was nothing short of miraculous for me. When you are led through the trials of life you ought to seek the explanations behind them. What are the subliminal messages being created for you?

Five simple things to embrace the messages and take massive action.

1. You must stop and pray.
2. You must listen and write down what you hear.
3. You must pray for the messages being received.
4. You must surrender to resistance.
5. You must act.

Three ways to Demand Your Presence.

1. Don't let your past define you- I could have easily used my past as a crutch to play the victim. What would it have done for me? The answer is nothing. It probably would have kept me from seeking the possibilities of true happiness. It could have kept me in the same circle of destruction. We all have a choice. A. Do you sit in your sorrow? Or B. Do you create a solution for yourself to produce different results? You are correct if you went with option B.

2. Never accept how other people define you- Individuals that know you from your past may not get over what they have witnessed about you. Sometimes they can't believe that someone can bounce back from a lifestyle of destruction. They may also anticipate how long it will take for you to mess it up again. Never let anyone have the final say on how you will live the rest of your life. Remember they are not you and they don't know what you aspire to do.

3. You could rewrite your story at any given moment- Our mistakes are the errors to pay closer attention to. It lets us know what works and what doesn't. The truth is, we can learn from our encounters. It provides the tools we need to move forward by correcting our actions, which gives us that open window of opportunity to create a new you. People reinvent themselves all the time.

We are all destined for greatness. When we experience all the emotions life has to offer, we become equipped with choices to decide what stays and what goes. That is the power of the ability to build our own legacies to leave for the next generation. Are you ready to demand your presence?

About the Author

Nicky Cuesta is a loving wife, and a mother to an amazing son. Her family drives the WHY in everything she does. As a Master Business Life Coach, Nicky helps to empower women to create their own dream lifestyle. Nicky does this by using all her platforms to highlight every area of the lives of those that connect with her. Nicky is on a mission to empower her community through her Building a Leadership Mindset Book, Podcast, Community & Coaching Program. She has assembled a powerful sisterhood with growth minded women called Ladies of Leadership "Demanding Our Presence" Community. Nicky's journey has been building for 20 years, but has recently taken flight within the last year. You can follow her journey on all her handles: https://linktr.ee/nickycuesta

Chapter 10 – Katie Escobar

"I will go before thee, and make the crooked places straight."
Isaiah 45:2

THE CROOKED PATH

The blue lines slowly appeared as I held my breath. For a moment, time stood still. As the unmistakable lines revealed themselves, it felt like the floor below me fell from its place. Panic. Dread. Disbelief. How could this happen to me?

Rewind a few years to a chastity conference by a well known priest. A news reporter pulled me aside and asked me some questions. "Just because everyone is doing it, doesn't mean I have to," I responded. Fast forward to the numerous pro life rallies, conferences, and debates. How could this same girl find herself in college facing an unplanned pregnancy? This is the story of my choice, my acceptance, and the wonderful ways it has changed my life.

I was born and raised Catholic. My faith was always important to me, and I sought to live it out to the fullest. High school was met with growing pains and peer pressure, but I stayed true to myself and my core beliefs. When it became time for college, I was intent on going to a school that would help me grow in my faith rather than lose it. I ended up at an orthodox Catholic school and further embraced the teachings of my faith. I wanted to study theology, get married, and become a teacher or do some type of mission work overseas. I even considered a religious vocation for a while. I didn't drink or do any of the stereotypical college things. However, there was a growing angst inside. My mom and dad met when they were in high school. My sister and her husband met in high school, and I grew up hearing of the young romance between my grandparents. As silly as it sounds now, I had an unconscious belief that I would meet my husband at a young age as well. Maybe my introverted and quiet nature was keeping me from meeting someone?

I ended up transferring schools and with the fresh start decided to go out more. I got involved with the party crowd and compromised my beliefs. I had a lot of fun, too much fun really, but I still did well academically. This period of life was only temporary, so why not enjoy myself? After graduation I would find a job and buckle down to work, I thought. I didn't even realize the hypocrisy that I was living. Here I was studying theology in a well known Catholic institution, but not living a virtuous, moral life. I met a guy at college amidst the hazy blur of parties and alcohol. I cared for him a lot, but his interest in me was inconsistent. Like the randomized dopamine hits of gambling, I was hooked. When he left the school unexpectedly, it confirmed that I was way more attached to him than he was to me. It was painful to accept once and for all that my feelings toward him were not reciprocated.

Over the summer before my senior year, I was reeling from this relationship and at a low point. I connected with an old crush from high school, and we began hanging out. In my mind this was a carefree way to pass time in the summer and to numb the brokenness that I felt before finishing my last semester. I had no intentions of pursuing anything serious with him, which is why the news of my pregnancy was such a jolt and so terrifying.

"This can't happen" was my initial reaction to finding out that I was pregnant. How could I make it not happen? My entire life flashed before my eyes. Your whole life really can change with one decision. As a pragmatic person, I immediately considered my options: keep the baby, adoption, or abortion.

I knew that no matter how desperate I was feeling or how much this felt like the end of the world, abortion was not an option. But would I be strong enough to uphold my beliefs? How would I tell my family? My friends? People would judge me. Unable to cope with these questions, I got in the car and drove around. Where to go? How could I escape? I actually ended up in a cemetery. Perhaps I was drawn to the macabre atmosphere because it represented how I felt inside. While driving through the cemetery the song "How to Save a Life" came on the radio. I knew this song was directed at me and my unborn child, and it was the first of many validations along the way that God was watching out for me in this situation.

I finished my last semester only telling my roommate about my pregnancy. Ironically, she had been studying crisis pregnancies as part of a course for her mental health major, so she had resources on hand that helped support me. I went home for Thanksgiving break knowing I had to tell my parents. Honestly, that was the scariest part. I didn't want to hurt or disappoint them. When I finally mustered the courage to say "Mom, I need to tell you something" she responded with, "Honey, are you pregnant?" Call it mother's intuition, but somehow she knew. As anguishing as that moment was, I was so thankful that she said the words so that I didn't have to. I broke down in tears, and she held me. Although this was not what my parents wanted for me, they were supportive. Active in pro-life ministries for years, it forced us all to "put our money where our mouths were" so to speak.

Thankfully, I was scheduled to graduate a semester early so I was only in school during my first trimester. I came home after graduation and took some time to figure out what to do. Once I accepted the reality of my situation, I knew it was no longer about me or what I wanted. I needed to make decisions that were best for my child. Abortion was off the table, and as much as I hated the thought of adoption, I wasn't sure I was ready to raise a child. I begrudgingly went to visit an adoption agency to get all the facts and make the most informed decision possible. This meeting would solidify in my mind that I was going to raise this child no matter the struggles ahead. I resolved that my child's existence would not be a "mistake". I began working at a daycare center and was charged with taking care of the infants. I got really comfortable taking care of babies during this time. I always saw that time as God preparing me for what was to come. The woman I worked with was a great support and even threw me a baby shower. (Crazy side note, she later became my son's kindergarten teacher through a divine set of circumstances.)

Another validation came at my twenty-week ultrasound. As my baby got a clean bill of health and we heard "it's a boy!," he gave a clear thumbs up gesture. The doctor excitedly snapped a photo and captioned it "thumbs up". This encouraged me that I was, in fact, making the right decision, and that God was watching over us. I can't express how much I needed this sign as I was still filled with much apprehension and fear of how all of this would work out.

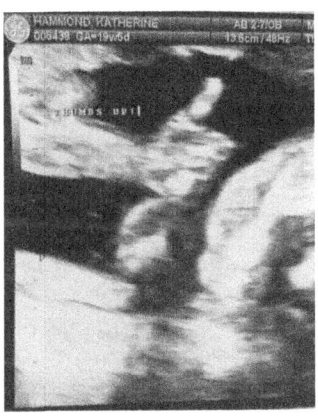

The months passed, and I anxiously awaited the birth of my son. A month before my due date I was spending time with his biological father. It was late evening, rainy, and out in the country. Something in my gut told me not to drive that night. I called my parents and said that I would spend the night there.

About an hour after falling asleep I awoke with the sudden urge to use the bathroom. My water broke and was tainted with meconium (a sign that the infant is in distress). I called the doctor, who told me to wait until I had contractions closer together and for a longer period of time before coming in (this was awful advice). I immediately started having horribly painful contractions and began throwing up from the pain. Thinking we still had a lot of time, we drove to my parents house.

Upon seeing my condition my dad called 911. The worst pain of my life ensued and Noah was rapidly born. On our couch. Delivered by my mom. Gray. Not breathing. My initial thought was he was going to die right there. That this whole situation would end with one cruel twist. The medics finally arrived about a minute later (they had made a wrong turn and were told there was no imminent delivery) and put an oxygen mask on to get him to breathe. They rushed us to the hospital, and the doctor gasped when she saw him. He was whisked away from me. I awoke the next morning in the hospital by myself traumatized by what had happened and not knowing if he had survived the night.

By the grace of God, he was alive. He was only 3 lbs 14 ounces and suffered from intrauterine growth restriction. For whatever reason, he had stopped growing and made a last ditch effort to survive. He was stable but still had a host of challenges before him.

The next few weeks were spent in a stressful limbo as he stayed in the NICU, and I was released from the hospital. As anyone who has been through a NICU experience will tell you, it is physically and emotionally draining. His tiny body was hooked up to all sorts of cords and monitors, so holding him and changing his diaper was intimidating to say the least. I remember thinking how glad I was that I had the experience at the day care center all those months. A preemie baby is another level of challenge, but I felt relieved that I was used to changing numerous diapers every day. He made slow, but steady progress, and was finally able to come home seventeen days later!

Throughout my entire pregnancy and the first year of his life, I was idyllically hopeful that things would work out with his biological father. I wanted my son to grow up in a two parent household. However, as time went by, it became evident that that wasn't going to happen. Our backgrounds and worldviews were completely different, and we had different expectations about raising a child. He made decisions that were not congruent with someone who wanted to provide for a child. He always wanted me to take Noah to him, but he didn't make the effort to come visit us. At first I did this because of my desire for things to work out, but then I started to realize that I was not respecting myself or my child. Actually, it was probably more based on a fear of things not working out. What would happen then? I didn't want to deal with custody arrangements or doing it all alone. Furthermore, he wasn't contributing anything financially. One day I had gone to see him and upon leaving I mentioned he should start contributing some money. He didn't say a word and just walked away. This silence spoke volumes and became a defining moment for me as I realized this was not someone that I could count on let alone be in a relationship with. I ended the relationship and eventually gained sole custody.

Originally the news of my pregnancy was one of fear. But as time went on, most of these fears didn't come to fruition. While my parents did not condone the circumstances of my pregnancy, they were always supportive and loved Noah immensely from the start. He blessed my family in many ways and brought so much joy. For several years after his birth, I wrestled with what was God's will for my life. Had I messed up His plans for me? One day I realized I no longer knew what my future "would be" plans were and that the life I was living was indeed the life I was meant to live.

Reflecting on this period of my life, I can identify several lessons that I carry with me. First and foremost, hold yourself to high standards, but give yourself grace when you fall. I felt guilty for a long time about my choices that led to an unplanned pregnancy. I beat myself up for not living up to the standards that I and, most importantly, God had set. I learned that none of us is perfect and we will all fall at times. It's how you pick yourself up that matters. Ask God for forgiveness and then forgive yourself!

As women, I think we all have a deep down fear of ending up alone. This fear leads us to accept being treated in ways that are less than we deserve. At some point along the way, I realized that my desire to be treated right had to be stronger than my fear of being alone. I started using this idea as a way to gauge if I should be in a certain relationship or not. You are worth more than you know and must not settle for less. This made all the difference as I moved forward and eventually met the man I married.

Finally, God can make even crooked paths straight. Things were not easy, but I put everything back in God's hands and trusted Him to take care of us. I wish I could say trusting

God with my future was a one-time thing, but I had to do it over and over and over again. When I look back, I can see how He was working in my life even when I didn't see it. Even when I felt like I had turned my back on Him, he still worked out all things for my good (Romans 8:28). At this point in my life, I can't even imagine my life without my son, and I am thankful that God blessed me with him.

I used to meditate on the circumstances of Mary being young, unmarried, and pregnant with Jesus. God did not abandon them, but entrusted them to Joseph. I used to joke that I would end up with a Joseph one day. Now, sure enough, I am happily married to Jose (Spanish for Joseph) with four more children. The love story between my husband and I would not have been the same without my son. He is an essential part of our family, and his younger siblings adore him. The original feeling of going off course and getting back on track is gone. I am where I am supposed to be, and Noah is meant to be here as well. What initially seemed like the end of the world ended up as the biggest blessing, and I can't wait to see all the amazing things he does with his life!

About the Author

Katie Escobar is a wife, mother of 5, and ESOL teacher turned homeschool mom. She lives in Maryland and enjoys the outdoors, reading, dancing, and caring for her domestic church. She can be contacted at khammond9285@yahoo.com

Chapter 11 – Karen Wigent

"Trust in the LORD with all thine heart; and lean not unto thine own understanding. In all thy ways acknowledge him, and he shall direct thy paths."
Proverbs 3:5-6 KJV

LOCK ARMS WITH JESUS

My story starts, as most do, as a happy little girl. I would say I had the best parents anyone could ask for. Even today my mother is still my best friend, and I cannot imagine my life without her. One year, I was in a Christmas pageant, and I was playing an angel. My mother gave me a gift of a beautiful brooch in the shape of a candle. She pinned it to my angel gown that I was wearing, and I remember how happy I was. I proudly showed it to my grandmother and father.

My grandmother was faith-driven and worshiped Jesus. I remember she also had a gift for me that day. I received a beautiful lighted golden candle to hold as I walked down the aisle at the pageant. My father looked at me and proudly said, "Shine little girl. The world will be watching." I was proud of my part in the play. I held my candle and walked down the aisle singing, "This little light of mine. I'm going to let it shine."

That was one of my cherished memories, and that's kind of how my life began at approximately five to six years of age. I lived in a family who loved me and loved Jesus although I remember in the months and years that followed; the light would soon dim.

I was hurt as a young child. As I grew older, through the age of ten, things began to happen that invaded my privacy. I won't go into detail, but they destroyed my innocence. I still remember the fear as I walked into my father's barn or whenever I got into "the vehicle", the fear overwhelmed me. I didn't know how to tell anyone what was happening. I didn't tell anyone what was happening to me, but my grandmother could sense something was wrong. She noticed one day; I was frightened to walk upstairs.

She took me aside and asked, "Honey, are you alright?" I was afraid to talk. I did mention to someone I did not want to ride in a car. I could not bring myself to tell my grandmother, mother or father what had been happening. I suffered from nightmares and experienced awakening in dark shadows of pain. The struggle in my mind, I did not know whether to be quiet or shout. I remembered my grandmother always telling me, "To lock arms with Jesus and everything would be okay." She told me this often hoping to reassure me and I would no longer be afraid. Little did I know how powerful that phrase would mean to me at that young age. It connected later in my life, as I got older.

I grew up learning to also hide behind my smile. Deep inside, however, I felt such a deep sadness. I could be in a crowd of people and still feel isolated and blue. I could not seem to connect with a lot of people. Because of my younger years, I was very hesitant to start enter the dating scene. It took me years to adjust to the feelings of being vulnerable. I wanted my father to know the pain I carried. I kept thinking one day I would tell him, but he passed away before I could say. Losing him before I could share my pain with him felt like a beautiful chain that had lost a link. Nothing made sense, nothing connected anymore. I didn't even feel connected with my Jesus Christ. I found love and joy only in my horse "Patches". Patches became my only friend with every hug I gave him. I found more strength and security. It was then I remembered whose I am. I made a conscious effort to strengthen my relationship with Jesus because I knew I needed a higher connection that would only come from Him.

In years to come, after having children of my own, I tried to protect them as much as possible. I held on so tight to them, that I smothered them. I was an overprotective mother. Today, I still struggle with leaving my grandchildren out of my sight.

Throughout my life, I felt increasingly isolated and sad. Unless you experience trauma of any kind, no one understands that horrible hollow hole feeling. I did experience "many" moments of happiness, but those moments came and went. There was a point in my life nothing that used to make me happy and excited about living stayed with me. I learned to go through the emotions of what I felt I must do and felt the pointlessness of it all. I did not know why I was feeling this way. I just know that I felt most alone.

I met a friend who had an awesome heart. She had a way of always complimenting others, making them feel special, and hoping to get the same in return. You see, she also learned to bury her pain in different ways. Little did I realize, she understood what I was going through. I was unable to meet with her when she called to set up an appointment. I always regretted that.

I also was not able to recognize the call for help from my friend when I should have. The results were devastating. I felt such a heavy loss in my heart and felt broken. If only I had connected with my friend that was feeling so lost, I would be talking to my friend now instead of wiping my tears away because I did not see the signs. I was so disconnected and used to being isolated in my sadness.

I often think about her and how alone she must have felt. It may have felt like she had a black shadow sitting on her shoulder whispering into her ear. While my friend was trying to live her life, her illness pushed her into a corner away from everyone else. I am sure this is how she felt, but she was not alone.

Unfortunately, depression can strike any of us at any time. Depression can make us very isolated. It makes us believe we are alone. The reality is people that reach out for help do not really know what their own needs are, so they stay quiet. They feel that they must figure it out alone. Most often, the results are not positive. In fact, one of the characteristics of depression is how divisive it can become. In our world today, mental illness has been on the rise more than ever.

We all have been dealing with a sense of disconnection lately, some more than others. It has taken considerable strength to come to terms and be honest about my feelings; about what had happened. My wish for the world is that no one should go through any of this alone or at all. I sense so many others are in pain when they do not have another person to talk to. I wish I could have recognized the signs and made a connection to help my dear friend. I am not going to let her sacrifice be for nothing. This was my wake-up call. I decided to make life worth living for us both. I had to follow God's plan for me. I had to do something positive to turn my pain around and honor my friend.

I cannot shake off the memories of the hurt and pain I experienced as a child. It is like a deep root covered with scars. But I remember what my grandmother told me so long ago, and I lock arms with Jesus to ease the pain. I also continue to search my heart for something…I don't know what it is. I feel like I am missing a piece that will free me from these insecurity and painful memories.

I signed up to take a class which I anticipated helping me become a stronger me. As the instructor was speaking, I heard the word "lock arms", which took me back to my childhood days. It inspired me to create a pendant to resemble how I was feeling. My instructor, Elena Rodriguez, still supports me and is behind me today.

As I sat thinking and sketching a very rough draft of a unique pendant, all I kept thinking about was what I could do to help others escape their dark world of disconnection and isolation.

And let me tell you, it took incredible strength to be honest about it all and do the work required to even get this project off the ground. I almost quit. My father passed away, and that connection was broken. I found myself once again, locking arms with Jesus because I knew then, as I know now, tomorrow is not promised.

It was totally out of my comfort zone, but I felt like God was leading me. What I learned in this process of designing this piece of jewelry is, the one truth I came to realize is that I am not alone in my pain. And people need to know they are not alone either. People need connection. They need to know where there are others out there who see them, who know how they felt, and who can help them get through this.

Through my own horrible experience, my heart has been empowered to help lift others out of their pain and darkness. I created my website, "Time 2 Connect" when I realized that so many others were fighting with their own guilt, their own battles when it comes to mental health or losing someone they loved because of it.

I don't know about you, but I have struggled each day since that moment when I was too late to connect with my friend. I want to be there to help others and ease their struggles. It is a sensitive subject I know, but we can show love, respect, support, and connection without saying a word by "locking arms" and standing together so that we can each do our part to help and support each other. Find out first in your heart who you are and then connect with someone in need.

No one should ever feel alone and helpless. With "Time 2 Connect", I feel that I have opened the gateway to healing in some small way. Wearing a locking arms pendant around my neck each day brings a feeling of joy and hopefully understanding to the person that I miss today. This is why I started the "Time 2 Connect Movement". I want everyone who is going through a hard time to know they're not alone. That is why I have designed a beautiful and unique pendant to wear proudly in honor of those affected by mental illness and to serve as a reminder that there is a community who sees you and supports you. We are all worthy of love and want to be valued. I have joy in my heart today knowing who I am.

I find myself once again, locking arms with Jesus because I know tomorrow is not promised. Please don't let your time run out. My hope is you know there is a higher power and I believe it's Jesus.

Lock arms with the only one that can bring you to a place of peace in your life.

The one is Jesus Christ.

About The Author

Karen Wigent gives credit for her strong will as a Warrior Woman to her mother, her deep faith to her father and grandparents in heaven, her husband that stands beside her and holds her up when she falls; her sons for putting up with a mother that loves so dearly she didn't want to let go, her friends that listen to her rattle and brings out the best of her laughter and tears, and her grandchildren that brings her the biggest smiles to her heart.

 Karen and her family live on a farm in Indiana. She enjoys spending free time searching for unique art, listening to music, reading, walking in the woods, and sitting by campfires with her family and friends.

Karen's passion led her to create the website, "Time 2 Connect." She realized so many others were fighting with their own guilt, their own battles when it comes to mental health or losing  someone they loved because of it. Click on the following QRCode and visit her website to learn more.

Chapter 12 – Whitney Marie

The woods are lovely, dark and deep,
But I have promises to keep,
And miles to go before I sleep,
And miles to go before I sleep.
By "Robert Frost"
Robert Frost, "Stopping by Woods on a Snowy Evening

THE GIFT THAT KEEPS CALLING

Have you ever felt like you weren't good enough? This is a story of how a teenage girl took on a task and fresh start, new birth of possibilities and faith. Through years of starting over and getting it wrong, I'm still here to tell her story.

I remember the tiny room filled with colorful objects and a mind full of possibilities. The open window allowed the wind to fill the room with the scent of rain and autumn. A tiny flip phone played a jazz ringtone on repeat. There lay a young girl in her bed, in a coddled position with her cell phone laying on top of her belly right in place enough for her unborn baby to enjoy the soft melodies that played through the tiny phone speaker as the unborn kicked to the sounds that made him joyful.

This 13 year old girl had been scared and became pregnant with no plan or knowledge of how to raise a child. She knew that this baby would have a better start because she was going to make it possible. Not sure how or where to begin, but people flooded us with love and direction. My Infant and I were both housed in several foster homes until we found a good home where we could thrive.

I've always been so afraid of rejection and starting over because of the unknown and the anxieties that come with the thought of losing control, in addition to moving. I'd spent the majority of my teenage life on the go, running away from abuse, and in and out of foster care. At 16 years of age, I moved into my own apartment with my son. I still remember our moving day. I brought our clothes and boxes filled with journals and old poems because they were dear to me. We opened the doors to our new temporary place, and the windows were as big as the sun, which shined through my apartment, and it came fully-furnished. Instantly, I felt safe and overwhelmed with gratitude because GOD had provided a place for me once again. A place I could truly call my own and teach my son all the things I know and more. A place where we can learn, and where he would feel no judgment, but have the freedom to express himself in ways that I had never been able to. A place where I can be free to be myself and dream.

I continued to go to school while raising my toddler which wasn't as bad as I thought it would be because we had been blessed with our own special community. I've always enjoyed learning but was rejected from my peers because I was a young mom. It was hard for them to take me seriously and like me because I had done the unspeakable and that was to have a kid so young.

Some of my teachers didn't even believe that I had the ability to learn because I was so far behind academically. I showed up every day trying my hardest, and I passed every class except math. I just needed a little more help from teachers, However, that was not a priority for my math teacher. Although I had a community of people who blessed me, I didn't have a community of teachers that were willing to help me get to the next level. I wanted nothing more than to excel at raising a child, but also earn my diploma and walk across the stage.

During my 11th grade year, I sat in math class with my hands up ready to answer a question. I knew the answer to this question, and I was so eager to answer it, but when the teacher called on me, I blurted out the wrong answer. I was so embarrassed and the class laughed and whispered, "Dummy."

I looked my teacher dead in his eyes, and I couldn't believe the rage I saw as he turned red and yelled, "Are you stupid or something!". I can laugh at this now because I still don't know what caused me to blurt out the wrong answer when I knew the correct answer. My teacher uttered those horrible words and I simply put my head down as tears began to form.

Here I was in the 11th grade and placed in a lower math class. I thought to myself "I'm too far behind". I remember my health teacher said to me "Whitney you should just go and get your GED because you are too mature for school." Those words were playing in the back of my head as I walked down to the principal's office to get my dismissal from high school entirely. I was already feeling ashamed and defeated. As I sat down with my principal, I was hoping to receive some words of wisdom and to be stopped from making one of the worst possible decisions.

Maybe I just needed a pep talk to keep on going, but instead I heard one of the most hurtful phrases ever uttered. He said, "You're finally doing it, huh?" I couldn't believe that he could say that to me as a student and not offer any assistance before he shook his head and signed my release paper. I wondered if the lead poison I was exposed to as a child had affected my learning abilities. Were my teachers aware of my disadvantage? Needless to say I left school with my head held high and went straight to work. With New beginnings and a gift I can use to develop self-esteem and overcome fear, the gift of writing and delivering specially spoken word I can absolutely become great.

As a kid, I remember watching Def Jam poetry at midnight on Friday nights. I have been inspired by watching YouTube videos right after to keep up the excitement I had been feeling. After that, I'd stay up writing my own pieces and know that one day I would be on a stage just like the people who recite poems and inspire others to do the same. While staying in independent living, I was introduced to open mics and other platforms with artists all over Rochester, NY.

I had become so ecstatic that I couldn't even sleep the day before because finally there was an open mic and a community of artists that I could be a part of. It was a dream come true for me. I would stay up all night after putting my son down to sleep, writing and rehearsing my pieces so that I could muster up the courage to go on stage. When it was my time... The same feelings of when I was back in math class slowly took over, feelings of shame, guilt and being misunderstood. My mind would wander to "what are they going to think about this poem, am I embarrassing myself?" I had feelings of, "I mean nothing, no one is going to care."

Until 2007, I decided to be courageous and recited my first piece. The piece was dedicated to my 13 year old self. "if i could be her again" Instead of all of the intrusive thoughts and negative feelings, they were surprisingly empowering, I felt tension releasing in my shoulders. It was like something had taken over me. But I hated the anxiety I felt right before stepping out onto the stage. I just didn't believe in myself

Ready to take on the next show, over and over again right before I go on to recite my poem, I couldn't shake the feelings of doubt, guilt and shame. I thought I had overcome and battled through those feelings, but as I got better and as more opportunities arose, the louder those intrusive thoughts fluttered my brain.

I just needed something to calm my nerves. I realized that I needed wine to calm my nerves from the social interactions of speaking and performing. One glass of wine would help with my social anxiety and fear, until one glass of wine turned into five glasses and over time the embarrassment and bad habits took over, but the intrusive thoughts and feelings subsided. Instead of using my gifts to heal from my traumas, I used alcohol to cope.

I used alcohol to cope with break ups, being mistreated, feeling not good enough and just everyday life stress. I even used it to boost my confidence. I used it to cover up every scar.

I became so comfortable with wine and releasing my ambitions as I went on stage with no feelings of fear. I felt invincible and tried to conquer and prove myself to an audience, and convince them, and myself that I matter, I'm intellectual and I can be exceptional with performing and using my gifts.

For me, performing was a way to release all of the emotions that I had held so dear for years. It was a way for me to release my trauma and heal. Acting, reciting my poems and sharing my story meant so much when I thought it mattered, but I just couldn't get past the guilt and shame I felt after writing. To go back to a place that hurt. I was ashamed of dropping out of school, not attending college, being a young mom and not being able to live the life that I aspired to live.

With that, I didn't see a way out of my situation. So I stuck to drinking alone and daydreaming of being great without truly putting in the effort required to change my life, without learning to actually deal with my hurts and heal from the cards I had been dealt. It wasn't until my drinking got so bad, and I lost friendships and opportunities that I finally realized that I had a problem. I stopped showing up because

I knew that if my drinking went too far, I would most likely sabotage myself. I remember my father telling me that if I don't learn to live with my regrets and decisions when I get older, it will eventually catch up to me. He was right.

I grew up being told "Whitney nothing is wrong with you", or "Stop making excuses" when I really didn't feel ok. Pushing my feelings and trauma aside and not actually showing me any grace or what to do, I walked around like nothing was wrong. I was trying to be a strong friend and not actually reach out for help because I would be pushed to the side or considered not a good friend. I was trying to be a strong mother, and smile, smiling so much started to hurt.

I never saw therapy as a good outlet to use. Growing up, I always thought that if I went to any counseling sessions it meant that I was mentally ill. I was too prideful to admit that I wasn't okay. But when life got too hard to handle I reached out to my Doctor and was referred to A DBT inpatient group. Dialectical Behavior Therapy was where I learned how to reprocess my feelings and trauma without substances. The thoughts and memories of sexual, physical and mental abuse that I had experienced as a child became too much. I had developed a very dangerous coping mechanism.

In therapy, I learned about the importance of taking walks and not sleeping with the TV on. I even picked up my pen and started journaling. Who would have thought that journaling before bed could release so much mental baggage?

Somehow, I had compartmentalized and buried my trauma too deep. I didn't know that I was afraid of feeling discomfort. All I needed to do was just learn to love myself a little more. I needed to forgive myself and stop looking for others to forgive me.

Learning healthy habits to deal with daily stress has helped. Hiking gave me a whole new outlook on life. From being outside and smelling the fresh air to appreciating the beautiful surroundings. I learned that forgiving yourself is a powerful tool when life gets too rough. Giving yourself time to feel is a form of self care. Going to therapy doesn't mean you are weak. Not finishing school didn't mean my life was over, and needing a break from life doesn't mean you have checked out.

I once read an article called "The Dangers Of Suppressing Emotions" By: Claudia M. Elsig MD. In the article, she states "How suppressed emotions stay in the body. The effects of suppressed emotions include anxiety, depression and other stress related illnesses that can oftentimes lead to alcohol and substance abuse." When our feelings are just too big to handle alone, we tend to go looking for something to help. I know that taking a walk, or counting to 100 doesn't always help when you are in the thick of things, If you can develop healthy daily habits, you might find better ways to cope. I had gotten so out of control with myself that I talked myself into a pit.

What do you do with feelings of being Inadequate?

Oftentimes, we feel like we were not good enough, or our words, presence and feelings don't matter. We may often feel rejected or unwanted.

We have a fear of letting our light shine and in most cases we feel trapped. We say to ourselves, "it doesn't matter any-way, or I'm not going to show up because I don't want to be judged and laughed at."

The fear of being rejected and not heard can come from many different things. Maybe you were rejected and picked-on as a kid, or experienced some form of sexual, physical emotional abuse, and you didn't have an outlet or were too afraid to speak up. I was taught to not speak unless spoken to, and that phrase replayed in the back of my mind when I wanted to speak up for myself.

GOD is calling on you to awake the gifts he has given to you and no substance or storms can stop His call. You are created from the Most High, and you are too important, too great not to shine your light. You have a testimony for a reason.

Not only did I overcome abuse, being a high school drop out ("but now a Graduate"} and a teen mom, but I also over-came the guilt and shame that came with all of that. I had the chance to bring the most intelligent, artistic human into this world and raise him with all I had in me. The enemy wants you to feel like you are not enough, inadequate and fearful. Now, I've learned how to speak up for myself and process my emotions in a healthier way. By writing and journaling and speaking with other young women, I also use that as a way to cope, instead of 6 pm cocktails after work.

By changing my daily habits and knowing my purpose, I can walk into that purpose with no shame or guilt and most importantly, sober.

About the Author

Whitney Marie is a mother of one child who is Graduating High school with honors this year 2023! She currently hosts a podcast on Spotify called " Whitney Marie Life Line" where she talks about her life living with Anxiety and also Sobriety. She enjoys writing, reading and working with young mothers and women who are transitioning into a life of sobriety. She believes that healing is a lifetime journey but with the right support you can live a life of abundance. You can connect with her on all platforms "Whitney_QueenMarie" or by email Whitneymariego@gmail.com

Chapter 13 – Kathy Mincer

"For I know the plans I have for you," declares the Lord,
"plans to prosper you and not to harm you,
plans to give you hope and a future."
– Jeremiah 29:11

YOU CAN OVERCOME!!

I was brought up in a very unstable family. My parents were always fighting, separating repeatedly and always moving. I was never in the same school district for more than a year. That left me feeling very vulnerable and never able to build relationships.

I was blessed to have God- parents who were there for me. They took me to church on Sundays and that was a get away from all the drama.

My mom, myself and my little sister moved to Naples, NY in 1978. We left my other 2 siblings behind with our dad. That was devastating!!! It was a couple years before we were all together again.

On a good note, I would be in the same school until I graduated. I took to not so good patterns with boys my age thinking they cared. At the age of 17, my senior year I became pregnant. Needless to say, mom was not happy. My mom made an appointment at planned parenthood, and by my surprise it was not for a check up appointment. She set up a abortion. I ran out and called my god parents and within hours I was headed back to Pennsylvania with them.

Eventually, 4 months later mom let me come home and live with her. I was 1 of 5 pregnant girls in my senior class that. I had a beautiful baby girl in March of 1981 and went back to school and graduated.

After graduating, I got married to a guy whom I thought was the best thing that ever happened to me.

We had two boys, so by the age of 21, I was a mother of 3 children under the age 5. I was totally wrong about him; he was very abusive, verbally and physically. I was so scared because where is a mother of 3 to go to keep them safe. Back then there was no help like today.

Fast forward 6 years and I am still married. A friend invited me out for my birthday. I jumped at it. Called my sister to watch the kids and I went.

I let loose, met someone, and was gone for the whole weekend. It was a good feeling, but this started my journey of being introduced to drinking. I never drank before this weekend. Remember, I was a mom of 3 and never had time to do anything for myself.

When I went home, I had already decided to leave. My husband would not let me leave at first. Locked me in the house, and became physical. Finally he let me leave, but only with my daughter because she was not his.

I found a little studio apartment for my daughter and me. During all this I always held a job so I would be able to support myself when the time came.

I continued to see the guy I had met on my birthday weekend. Eventually we moved in together. My thinking was I'm finally in a good place, but drinking became part of my life.

We got married in 1991, I was only thinking about security. On my weekend visitation with my boys, I was changing their shirts and noticed marks on their backs. They did not go back to their dad's. After a while they asked if they could see him, not wanting to be the bad mom I let them with supervision. That was a mistake, he filled their heads with lies and told them to tell school teachers a bunch of lies, they ended up being pulled from us and put in foster care.

Because of my partying, I lost many jobs for not showing up, we lost our house because I did not pay the mortgage. My husband was so angry with me. My daughter was in a car accident, I was too hung over to go be with her at the hospital. Not a proud mom moment!!!

My husband got some DWI's, but the last one he was looking at prison. He decided to get into a program hoping that would help his case. That started a whole new drama in our relationship.He got this holy attitude!!! His sentence was reduced to weekends in jail, a breathing machine in our house, and probation. I was not able to have any alcohol in the home. I GOT AN ATTITUDE!! I yelled, "You did this, not me." I was being told I had to do this and that for him and be available when he needed me. I asked for a divorce!

I got my own apartment, worked and continued partying. I had met a guy at the bar and he was much more fun than my husband because I had someone to party with. That went on for months, until one morning I woke up and just did not feel well. I knew I needed medical attention. I could not get a hold of any of my children or friends. Then knowing that my husband was still on my emergency contact, I called him and he came to help me.

On the way to the hospital he was not nice at all. He said, "I was worth more to him dead than alive." With tears rolling down my cheeks, I knew that I had hurt him badly!!!

While waiting for a doctor, my husband said, "look there's a man with a mission." He noticed an elderly man with a big AA book. During my emergency room visit, I found out my blood pressure was dangerously high, so I was hospitalized for three days.

I had hit my bottom! I did a lot of thinking and praying. I made a huge decision that it's time to change my life around. My daughter had come to pick me up, and then she took me to my apartment. I mustered up the nerve to call my husband

and ask where the next AA meeting was. He hooked me up with another lady that took me.

Thursday night and I was walking into a meeting. Everyone there already heard my husband's story about our life. They were not nice to me at all! If I did not know about AA, I would have walked out. I was there to work on myself, not my husband. I decided to go to meetings that he did not attend, to heal me.

It was NOT easy, because he had so many people on his side. They put bets on me that I would not make it, which made it much harder. But I was determined!! I was not doing it for anyone else but me. For those folks not believing in me, I created a God box and when I heard negative comments from them, I would put their names in there for Him to take care of. I worked the steps with a couple of great women. God was my higher power!

During all this, I found out who my REAL friends were. I had to change people, places, and things in order to stay away from triggers. At times they still came up, but it was not worth picking up a drink and going down that road again. Instead I prayed, walked, or just went for a drive and jammed tunes.

Eventually, Matt and I started dating again. I told him I would like to not continue the divorce. He replied, "No you asked for it, so I'm going to give it to you." Ouch! We met at the courthouse to sign the paperwork together. The judge was shocked!

At this time he was almost 3 years sober and I had 6 months. We continued dating. Let me tell you this was a totally different relationship. We went to meetings and had a higher power, and prayed together. Then he was going to buy his sister's trailer and my lease was coming to an end at my apartment. So I needed to know if we were going to try to live together. He left me hanging, then decided we would give it a shot. When this was decided I had almost a year sober.

The one person who gave me the most negative comments saw that I was being true to my new life. He asked Matt, "When are you going to make your relationship true?" After I had a year of sobriety, Matt got on one knee and asked me to marry him again. He never did that the first time. We made plans to travel to Vermont to get married at the home of the founder of AA. We got married there on February 23, 2013.

While creating this new beautiful life, we started on a wellness journey. Getting sober brought out a lot of issues in me that the drinking and drugs were covering up. I was actually on medications and had breathing issues. A friend introduced us to Essential Oils, a natural way toward wellness. We educated ourselves, with the help of some great people, on how these little bottles of essential oils could help us with emotional, spiritual, and physical needs. We took baby steps on this Journey. In time we started sharing with families the tools we had, which in turn gave us a second income.

We always heard about building a vision board. We did it together and put it where we would see it everyday. We worked hard for fours years, I changed my career to caring for the elderly, and it happened that we closed our home up to care for my husband's friend, he was the one that was most negative to me, so he could stay in his home for the rest of life. That was powerful! We were able to get out of debt, and the last thing on the vision board was to buy a log home. We know the next thing that happened was ALL God.

We have a realtor on our business team and she knew our vision and that butterflies were my symbol, my mom loved them. Realtor said,"this is for you" make sure you go to the last picture, which was of a log home with 5 acres and with a stained glass window of a butterfly. I told her, "We are buying it!" Come to find out we could not get a traditional mortgage because the house didn't have water or sewer. It was a hunting cabin.

Matt and I decided maybe it was not our timing. I was taking care of this beautiful couple and they watched as we grew. They knew that we were trying for this, and when I told them we could not get the mortgage and why, they offered to give us the money.

We put in an offer, then went on a mini vacation to a Kingdom Bound a Christian event with many speakers and music. We decided that the only reason we would answer the phone was if it was the realtor. They accepted another offer. We were broken-hearted, but we continued to worship the rest of the weekend. On the way home a call came saying that the offer fell through and the log cabin was ours! Another God moment.

We ended up buying our home in September of 2018 and moved in April of 2019. Renovation of the cabin took a lot of work, but Matt has his own construction business. Thank goodness because we needed to have an addition put on the cabin. We were paying for both of our places. During this busy time we decided to get baptized together at our church, January, 2019.

We kept living our good life. Sometimes, I look at him, and say "who is this man?" "He" is Totally different.

"As of today", we are living a healthy lifestyle, sober almost 12 years, and have no desire to pick up a drink, drug, or cigarettes. Yes we quit them also. We have 3 beautiful grown children; who thank God, did not follow in our footsteps of drinking. They all have great careers and have given us 5 beautiful grandchildren. They are all teenagers and we are so grateful for their upbringing. I continue to care for the elderly, even hospice care. My husband has a great construction business, and we both have created a flourishing Health and Wellness business called BELIEVE. We have paid off our house. We live a very simple life on our mountain.

Despite my struggles and hardships I faced, I never lost my spirit and determination. My journey through alcoholism serves as a reminder that recovery is possible, and my strength serves as inspiration to all. My legacy will live on, reminding future generations of the power of hope, courage, and the human spirit. YOU CAN OVERCOME!

About the Author

Kathy Mincer is a wife, mother of 3 grown children and 5 grandchildren. She lives in the beautiful Finger Lakes of New York where she enjoys gardening, crocheting, caring for the elderly and sharing Wellness, Purpose & Abundance with her business BELIEVE Essential Oils You can learn more at her site by scanning QR code:

Chapter 14 – Elizabeth Cruz

"Proverbs 31 woman loading…"

STARBURSTS AND TOMATOES

I know you're probably thinking what a strange title for a chapter in a book. Especially a book about wonderful warrior women who wear invisible capes and have withstood so many traumatic events yet still find time to love, laugh, and smile.

And you're also probably thinking, or at least I would be… what a weird combination, a tiny, tasty piece of candy and a popular fruit/vegetable, what could they possibly have in common?

Truth is, they don't have anything in common for anyone in the world, except me. They are an integral part of my even considering to write this chapter and be a part of this project. They represent so much more than their nutritional value, or lack thereof. The minimal price tag for each one is not reflective of the immense impact these items have had on me. They are just a small ingredient, which I hope will become a full meal, warm and delightful, filled with love, kindness, and the spirit of giving. Like a recipe for your favorite comfort food laced with life lessons that I can pass onto my children.

Let's rewind a little bit before I share the vast effects of star-bursts and tomatoes.

My childhood was a bit rough, we were poor. My siblings and I were loved and almost always had food, but religion was such a focal point in our home, I think some very important life lessons were left off the menu.

I endured generational curses (that still haunt me today), sexual assault, physical abuse, and abandonment in multiple forms as a young girl. These events and the lasting effects play into every single relationship I have to this day. I've made tons of mistakes and even gave my parents hell as a teenager. I could write an entire book about the biggest sucker punch of my life, but this is not what my story is about. As a warrior woman, I survived the pain, fought for my sanity silently, and found beauty and positivity in heartbreaking circum-stances. I found strength and determination in the depths of my broken pieces.

I have hustled, struggled, grinded, and fought for my place in this world, predominantly on my own. Despite all my traumas, I've always kept a soft spot for the less fortunate or those in need, because I myself was less fortunate. Different people showed me love and grace along my journey, and I always desired to pay it forward. I believe that I have, but I believe there is more work to be done.

My career has taken me places I never knew I wanted to go and stretched me personally and professionally in ways that I did not believe possible. I am forever grateful for that. I feel like I have it all in many ways, however I am also aware there is a little something missing.

Which leads me back to starbursts and tomatoes….

Who knew these small items could evoke such overwhelming emotions in me and in others… and that feeling, those moments, I aspire to replicate whenever possible.

And for now, I'm not exactly sure how to do that on my own, but I will continue to raise my hand as a ready, and willing, participant when the opportunities arise. I also promise myself that I will try to create these opportunities for me and my family.

October 2012 Hurricane Sandy

I was in the movie theater when I got the call to be deployed to assist FEMA with those affected by Hurricane Sandy in New York. I didn't think twice, I have a ton of family in New York and I felt compelled to agree to this unknown assignment. I didn't know what exactly this deployment would entail, what my role would be, or where I would be staying. The only solid information I was given was that it would be a 45-day deployment.

Within a couple of days, my bags were packed, with sweaters, long johns, and all the warm clothes that I could find in my sunny, south Florida apartment. Anyone who knows me, knows I am not a fan of the cold, but off I went enthusiastically, to embark on this new assignment.

Once I arrived in New York, I quickly learned that my temporary new home would be a decommissioned Navy ship. To be quite honest I had mixed emotions about that, some of the higher ranking FEMA people were staying in hotels, and the worker bees were being treated like we were in the military. Bear in mind, I'm not fancy, I don't need much to get by, and I have nothing against military personnel, but I thought to myself this is going to be a strange place to live.

When I saw the size of the 'racks' for sleeping, I thanked God that I'm not claustrophobic. We had to line up for meals that were served prison-style by plopping a spoonful of food onto a metal tray. More often than not the shower area was flooded, which is highly unsanitary. The living conditions were not ideal, and some people requested to be sent home. That thought never crossed my mind. I signed up for this assignment, and I would gladly see it through to the very end.

Any sub-par living conditions we encountered were nothing in comparison to what the fine people of New York were experiencing. Many people lost everything, or, at the very least, they lost all the contents of their basements, memories and parts of the records of their family history.

It was very cold, and many residents did not have electricity/power/heat for months. How dare any of us complain or give up the mission?! An average day was 18 hours outside, walking, and knocking on doors. We educated residents on the FEMA process and helped them to apply for assistance. We offered useful information, support and when we had supplies, we offered blankets, MRE's and sometimes real food.

The days we could offer real food were few and far between, but I will never forget the day we had tomatoes to share. I knocked on the next door and went through our whole FEMA spiel. I could see the hopelessness in this woman's face, the look of despair, not knowing what to do next or how to start rebuilding her home and her life. Her despair hit me hard, so I excused myself for a moment to go to the supply truck to see what we had left. I saw a bunch of tomatoes and grabbed them. It wasn't much, hell, it wasn't even a proper meal, but it is all we had left to offer. I handed her the tomatoes trying to reassure her things would get better.

As I reached toward her, I watched our exchange in slow motion. We locked eyes and both burst into tears. She thanked me profusely. To have fresh tomatoes meant everything in the world to her. I will never forget her face. I will always remember that miniscule gestures of kindness can leave profound impressions on people and on my own heart and mind forever.

August 2021 Operation Allies Welcome

At 7am on a Sunday morning, my work phone rang. I ignored it because I was still in bed. The phone rang again, and this time, I looked to see who it could possibly be; it was my boss. I tried to clear my throat and answered. It was a call for another deployment.

This time it was to support the crisis in Afghanistan, which would be a 30-day deployment, and the location was to be determined. My marching orders were to be packed and ready to go by Tuesday. Based on my previous deployment experience, I knew I wouldn't get any specific answers or have any definitive duties until we were boots on the ground. I strapped in and hurriedly tried to meal prep for my family since I am the chef in our home.

After 26 hours of travel, rerouting to a different destination mid-trip and multiple flights we finally landed in Italy. We worked on a Navy base in conjunction with a multitude of other federal agencies. Our main goal was to receive refugees fleeing from Afghanistan and prepare them for flights and resettlement in the United States. My first day on duty we got oriented for the operation, housing system and responsibility my group would have in this massive undertaking.

All of this was happening during a deadly pandemic. Within a couple of hours, we got to observe one of those huge military aircraft land (the ones with no seats inside, the ones that can carry a jet or gigantic equipment). When they opened the belly of that aircraft; what I saw would change me forever.

I witnessed hundreds of men, women, and children, slowly exiting the aircraft. They were exhausted, scared, dirty and had a twinge of gratitude that they were fortunate enough to make it out alive. Some carried bags, boxes, broken luggage, kids dragged bags that were bigger than they were. Babies had on diapers that were obviously days old. Whatever they could carry in their hands when they escaped the turmoil of their homeland was all they had left in the world. Some carried nothing. It was heartbreaking to say the least, and yet, at the same time, it was hopeful.

Days and weeks went by as we prepared for our mission. We witnessed, laughter, tears, sickness, babies being born, desperation and anticipation of the new life that awaited them in a country that often categorized people from this region as terrorists. We witnessed utter poverty to the point we had to teach some people how to use a toilet as the only toilet they knew was a hole in the ground. We basically created a mini, makeshift airport on the naval base to process these refugees as passengers to bring them to America, the land of many dreams.

Finally, we got the green light to start sending out these flights, and our days became longer and longer. The 'airport' security process was challenging. Lines were long and moved at a snail's pace due to lack of space and equipment, among other things.

Language barriers were a huge obstacle. Translators were spread thin and running on empty, but still we persevered and processed thousands of people. During the processing of the passengers, I noticed kids being kids, antsy, tired, and unaware of their surroundings. I saw mothers struggling to keep track of multiple kids, bags, and documents. I wondered how I could help besides giving out high-fives and fist bumps to the children.

Around the corner from the makeshift security checkpoint, I recalled there was a table full of snacks and treats for us, the workers. I grabbed as many starbursts as I could and began giving them out to all the children in line. This small gesture made their day! Their reactions and smiles are etched in my mind. The nods of approval from the overwhelmed mothers was icing on the cake. A tiny morsel of juicy, fruity, chewy goodness made a huge transformation to so many kids whose lives were recently flipped upside down.

Once again a small simple act of charity filled me with a joy like no other.

So starbursts and tomatoes have become food for my soul, my recipe for joy.

I would like to share this recipe with you all and with my sons…

you don't always have to follow the recipe exactly; you can put your own twist on this incredible dish we call life -- by being a leader.

even when you mess up a dish, you can try again and you can master it—by persevering and remaining faithful.

you can express yourself in the kitchen by being creative and thoughtful about what components you put into a meal-- by thinking outside of the box.

you can be intentional about preparing a new meal, it can lead to stimulating and undiscovered flavors—you can find joy in unexpected places.

you can gain knowledge and experience by seeking opportunities to break bread with those less fortunate—by being gracious and compassionate to people and being open to new ideas.

you can share a meal with a friend or a stranger-- by being kind therefore impacting the lives of others.

you can show gratitude for the food in your refrigerator—by being thankful for what you have, and remembering some people have never tasted starburst before.

- you should share this recipe with everyone you encounter-- by acknowledging that while money can certainly make life easier it cannot fill your heart with this type of joy.

Chase and choose joy.

And last but certainly not least--remember to pray before you eat, All Praises to The Most High!

About the Author

Elizabeth Cruz is an International Aviation Inspector for Homeland Security. She lives in Florida and enjoys traveling, cooking, the beach, music and any outdoor adventure with her family.

Chapter 15 – Desiré Cruz

For I know the plans I have for you declares the Lord,
plans to prosper you and not to harm you,
plans to give you hope and a future.
– Jeremiah 29:11

PIECE BY PIECE WE ARE MADE INTO A MASTERPIECE

"Why Me?" These were the two words I leaned into most of my life. Pretty depressing I know. To be fully transparent, it was more than just two words that I would continually bark at God for years... it was an entire lifestyle and mindset that consumed me.

Growing up, my family struggled with many areas to be considered "successful". We had struggles with money, physical health, and mental health. We also had generational curses that were repeated rather than eliminated from the family line. These included poverty, effects of unhealed trauma, fixed mindsets, addictive personalities, and unhealthy communication skills. I loved my parents and my siblings, but I always felt like we were just stuck in this repetitive cycle and couldn't win.

It seemed to always be one thing after another that my parents were trying to figure out in order to just survive in Cape May, New Jersey. They had four kids, living paycheck to paycheck with only one vehicle. My parents both worked extremely hard for years but could never get ahead. I specifically remember when I was a little girl hearing my dad cry in the bathroom hysterically because of the financial pressure that was put on him as the man of the family. I'll never forget how that made me feel. We were living in an area of the country that was expensive to raise a family. Eventually it got bad enough where we had to use a kerosene heater in our living room for our source of heat and hot water. Together there were nights in the winter where we "camped out" in the living room to stay warm. I also remember connecting a bright orange extension cord over to the neighbor's house so we could have electricity. My mom was in retail her whole life for employment, which included all kinds of scattered hours,night and day shifts, and working every weekend. I deeply missed having her actually home while I was growing up. I remember at such a young age feeling so bad for my parents and constantly questioning why they had to face all of this. On the other hand,my child brain also would remind me that my friends were living in million-dollar homes, having two luxury cars, fridges full of amazing things to eat, and me always asking myself, "Why me?"

After relentlessly trying to make New Jersey work, my dad came home one night and said, "we are moving to Marion, New York." Which meant, I had to leave behind my friends, my school, and my extended family, who I was really close to. I spent the next couple days after the announcement crying to my best friends and in the back of my mind wondering, "Why me?" I went from the beaches to the cornfields. I was devastated, and angry. Now, becoming a true teenager at the age of 15, I felt completely lost.

I needed to readjust to learning all things about the country since the beachlife was over. I began learning how to ride four-wheelers, hunt, fish, and ride lawn mowers. Most importantly…learning what a great bon-fire party included. Beer, liquor, marijuana, cigarettes, and country boys… specifically Peter Ververs. My first puzzle piece.

I began dating Pete when I was 16. I felt like he was the only one in the entire world who knew me, who listened to me and loved me for who I was. He accepted me and my family along with our flaws. He was someone that I smiled with and had fun with. We did many major milestones together. We went to prom together, got our drivers licenses together, had our first jobs together, graduated together, and moved in with each other as soon as I turned 18. We had plans on getting married and having children. Plans to live a "successful life" I promised myself I would have. And it was exciting!

Unexpectedly, one day I began having a lot of pain. It led to an abnormal pap smear and was told from the doctor that day that there was a high chance I could never have children. I specifically remember that night Pete's face changed. He later confessed to me in the kitchen of our house, (both of us around 19) that he loved me more than life, but couldn't marry someone who couldn't have children. I remember instantly sobbing because his face just seemed to clearly express his full barrier in continuing a relationship with someone like me. There goes my perfect life I thought, instantly thinking of my victim mindset, "Why me?"

We prayed the doctors were wrong, and we continued our relationship happily and continued hoping for years. Oddly enough, on my 21st birthday I took a pregnancy test to find that I was pregnant! As you could imagine, my 21st birthday looked very different from most people. Pete and I could not believe it! His face changed back to the Pete I remembered. Glowing, and smiling ear to ear; knowing he could now be a father with the woman he loved. We told everyone! Pete and I were overflowing with joy! He began saving money from each paycheck for a ring. Together we picked out this beautiful cherrywood crib with his mom and created a nursery that was painted lavender purple with a butterfly theme. It was everything I could have ever asked for in a nursery. His face when the technician said, "it's a girl" is like a snapshot permanently stuck in my mind. He was overflowing with fulfillment. We decided to name her Haleigh Jade Ververs. Her due date was December 25, 2006... A Christmas baby! It was exactly how I wanted my life to look. I was so proud of us. My pregnancy was extremely smooth, and I was beginning to look very pregnant. I was at the end of my eighth month when Pete came home and said, "I am going to Sam's party to celebrate his birthday, and it will be my last party for a long time since the baby is coming soon." I encouraged him to have fun and be safe because I knew he would be drinking.

Around 2 am, I woke up in the middle of a dead sleep with this terrible gut feeling. I saw Pete was still not home and it was unlike him. I called Sam's house, and he yelled at me to never call that late again. I explained Pete still was not home, and I was very worried. Within a minute of him hanging up on me, I saw red lights flashing into my window. It's strange to say it now, but I instantly knew then something was very wrong with Pete. The gentleman who hung up on me called back and said Pete wasn't sleeping on the couch like he thought he was. My heart sank. Pete decided to walk home that night because he had drunk a couple beers. He was killed in a hit and run on October 22, 2006 in Marion, New York on the same back country road with no street lights where we lived. Those flashing red lights were the scene of the accident that I could see out the window of our home.

I called my best friend's husband at the time, and he drove me to the scene of the accident. I collapsed in the middle of the road sobbing, pregnant, after hearing from the state trooper that it was Pete who was hit and killed in a hit and run. I swear one of the first things I did, overcome with anger and sadness, was to scream at God, "Why me?" We worked so hard to have a different life, a happy life. How could this happen to us? To a man like Pete? I felt like my child and I were somehow being punished by God. I felt like I was born to just stay in that familiar dysfunctional cycle. It was exactly the life I did not want for my child.

Six weeks later, I was 21; and having my baby girl at Canandaigua Hospital all alone. We still did not know who killed

Pete. I had my mom come in the room with me to help deliver Haleigh, but it wasn't the same. I brought a picture of Pete with me to the hospital and placed it on a table so he could still see her when she was born. That photo brought me peace. I remember when she was born something inside of me changed. You see, I promised myself and Pete that I would give Haleigh the best mom and the best life, and I meant it.

After looking into her eyes once she arrived, I no longer thought "Why me?" For the first time in 21 years that I could remember, I felt called, and chosen, and experienced pure joy to be her mommy. I was a single mom for 5 years, and had my younger sister move in with me so we wouldn't have to do life all alone while mourning the death of my spouse. I slowly began working part time, putting myself through college, taking out student loans just to survive. I spent every minute with Haleigh, raising her to the best of my abilities. I didn't know much of the future, but I knew I was a good mom and that she had an incredible family who supported her. She was the next piece to my masterpiece.

I sought therapy, but was suffering with PTSD silently. Before I knew it, Haleigh began heading into Kindergarten. She was just learning how to ride a bike, and I was on my way to graduating college. I would take her every day after classes, and we would keep practicing her bike riding. Eventually, I took her to the park down the road so she could practice on the pavement. While I was there, I remember seeing this guy there with his little girl daily, and she was around the same age as Haleigh. He was around my age, and he was cute. We began talking, and sharing stories, and letting the kids play together at the park.

I found out later Jesse was a single parent, as well. His story ended in divorce, and his ex-wife was incarcerated for many years leaving his baby Mariah, who was three at the time, momless. I never thought I would meet anyone with such a dramatic story, until I met Jesse. For the first time in a long time, I felt as though someone understood a sliver of the pain I was experiencing.

Jesse and I began allowing our friendship to evolve into dating. He and Mariah were now my newest pieces to the puzzle. We enjoyed doing things together as a "family." Haleigh benefitted from having a male role model around, and Mariah now had a female role model. It was like God placed us divinely into each other's path. I will never forget when we were making dinner and saw the girls pray together outside at the table on the back deck. Jesse and I looked at each other and began to cry. We slowly began to trust in his plans. Years later, we got married in that same park. You see, He can take your broken pieces and still create a masterpiece.

Jesse and I graduated college together. Started our careers together, bought a home together. Raised our little girls together. But we wanted children together. So we began trying for a child. After years of waiting, we just gave up. But this time it was different. I didn't ask, "Why me?" We figured it wasn't in the plans.

Until one day four years later, I found out I was pregnant. We were so excited! We told everyone, had the ultrasound and a private gender reveal around Christmas time with all of our friends and family. We immediately named her, Faith Lucille-Marie Cruz. The next puzzle piece.

During my pregnancy I was in a lot of pain. I remember that pregnancy being nothing like when I was pregnant with Haleigh. I felt after I had the ultrasound things began to spiral down hill. I was at work around six months pregnant, sitting with my students at a lunch table, when suddenly I felt like I could no longer walk. I drove myself to the hospital and told them something was wrong! The doctors kept sending me home stating I had a fibroid that was the direct cause of the significant pain and it was "normal."

I was not heard until it was too late, and I went into preterm labor. I was screaming in pain. I kept feeling like I was going to faint because of how bad the pain was. I remember thinking that-I was not going to live through and neither was the baby. I had terrible thoughts cross my mind that my kids were, now, not going to have a mom, and my husband was losing his wife. I thought I would never cry out, "Why me?" again to God but here I was!!! I was driven by ambulance to Strong hospital in Rochester, NY. Even with Jesse along for the ride, I felt alone with God in that ambulance. I prayed intently. I begged him to let us live. Later that evening, Faith and I both survived the emergency C-Section.

I spent every second with my 1 pound premature baby girl, Faith. She was the smallest on the hospital floor. I was away from my kids and husband, sleeping at the Ronald McDonald House for 42 days. After very long, emotional days, I would leave the hospital to rest, and still would have to pump breast milk every 2 hours so she could have a chance to receive it. I was doing everything and anything that could help my baby girl.

After days turned into a month, I could see the doctors beginning to look at me differently. Their medical language started shifting in ways that were unfavorable to my daughter's life. Instinctually, I began feeling that Faith was not going to make it. God told me, like a whisper, to prepare me yet again for a significant loss. On the day she passed in my arms, I remember the overwhelming sense of loss my husband and I felt. Indescribably, I also felt instant peace. It was like God was comforting me during one of my most uncomfortable moments. I remember instead of blaming him for her death, I felt like He saved her from a life of hospitalizations and struggles caused from being on a ventilator. I felt as if he showed me a glimpse of heaven where she was. Pure and peaceful with no complications. I felt God whisper that Faith is with Pete now. Not to worry, they are in good hands.

Jesse can raise Haleigh while Pete raises Faith. The storyline he whispered made me sob like a child. It brought a sliver of light and hope that I had never fathomed about these two terrible memories I held onto for years. In a way I felt like it was God saying well done with the pieces that I have put before you.

I'm telling this story today to share the life lessons that were revealed to me through my life story. Before I leave this earth it's imperative for my kids, and other people to know that GOD IS REAL, even though we cannot see him. He has a way of showing up in EVERY piece of our lives so we are never alone even when we feel we are. The pieces we usually wish were never a piece; he takes and uses it to create a different masterpiece, one we could never imagine. He has shown me it's important to look ahead to the future pieces. To trust in the process, even when some pieces are very difficult to put together. Not to get stuck in just one piece. Because it can cause you to miss out on the grand reveal of the masterpiece HE has created for your life. Use his strength and pray for his guidance when you cannot figure out the puzzle. I can tell you I would not be the warrior woman I am today without each and every piece. The mother I am. The wife I am. The business owner I am. Trust me, one day, God will help you make sense of all the pieces when you cannot. Someday you too may even question Him, "Why Me?" I pray for peace in the revealing of your next puzzle piece.

About the Author

Desiré Cruz is a dedicated wife, and a mother of three beautiful girls. She has a passion for women empowerment, and loves exploring different cultures and food from around the world. She is the co-owner of Merge Worldwide, where she hosts live events for entrepreneurs from all over the country.

In these events we explore the power of combining community, networking, travel, and personal development. Please check out our Merge Worldwide Community where you can find recap videos of our previous and upcoming retreats or speaker competitions on the following platforms:

Facebook: Desiré Cruz/Jesse Cruz
Instagram: dcruz742014

MIC STORY SPEAKER COMPETITION
SAN ANTONIO, TEXAS
FEBRUARY 24-25, 2023

More Books From

   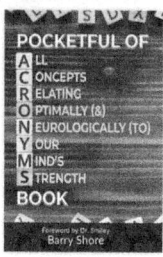 

www.PerfectPublishing.com

More Books From

www.PerfectPublishing.com

Made in the USA
Middletown, DE
31 May 2023

31792685R00113